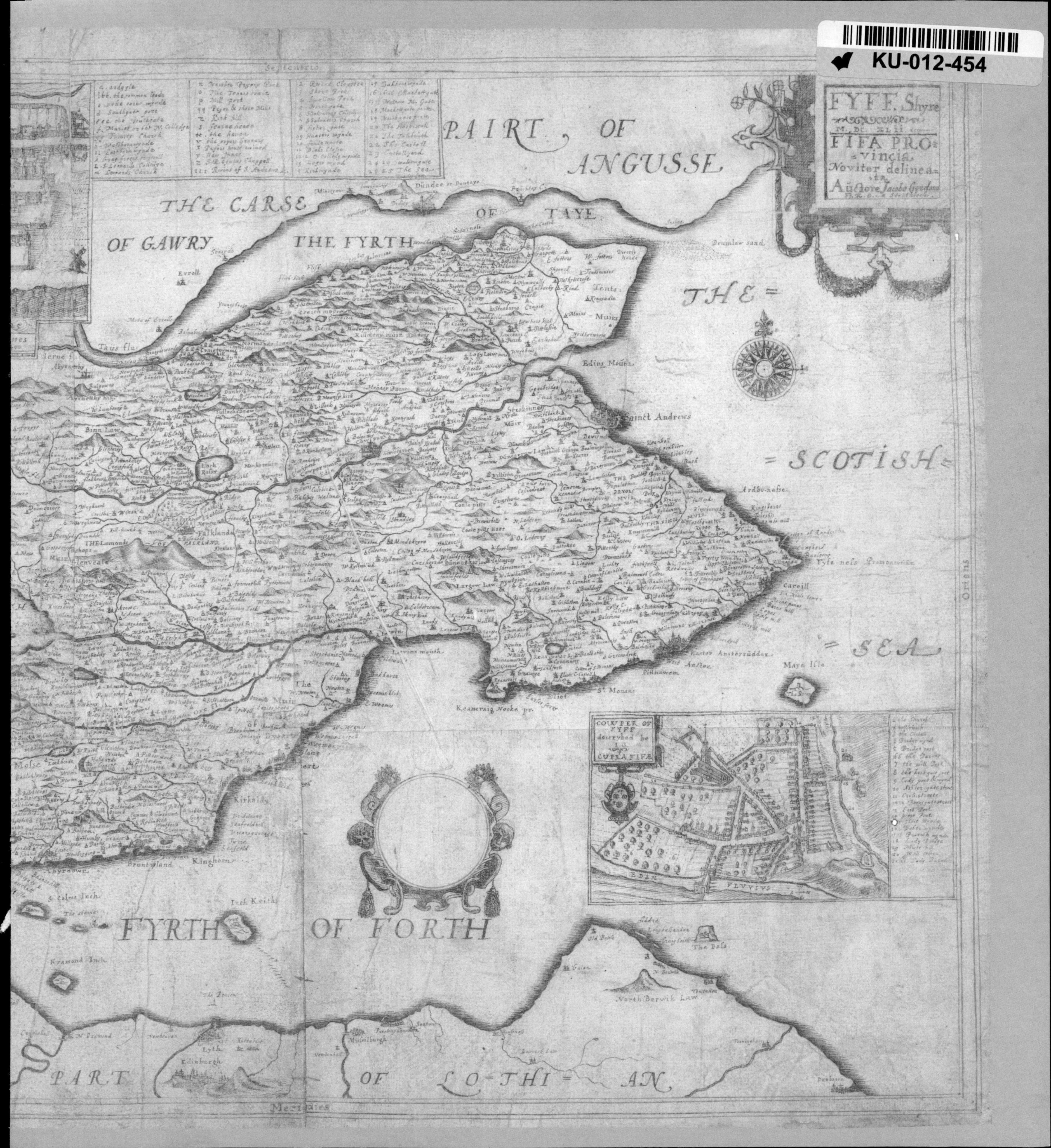
KU-012-454
FYFE Shyre
M. DC. XLII
FIFA PROvincia, Noviter delineata
Septentrio
PAIRT OF ANGUSSE
THE CARSE OF GAWRY
THE FYRTH OF TAYE
Dundee
Saint Andrews
THE SCOTISH SEA
Falkland
Kirkaldy
Kinghorn
Bruntisland
Fyfe-ness Promontorium
Easter Anstrudder
West Anstor
Maye Isla
Inch Keith
FYRTH OF FORTH
COUPER OF FYFE
FLUVIUS
The Bas
North Berwik Law
Kramond Inch
Lyth
Edinburgh
Mussilburgh
PART OF LOTHIAN
Oriens
Meridies

Fife from Above

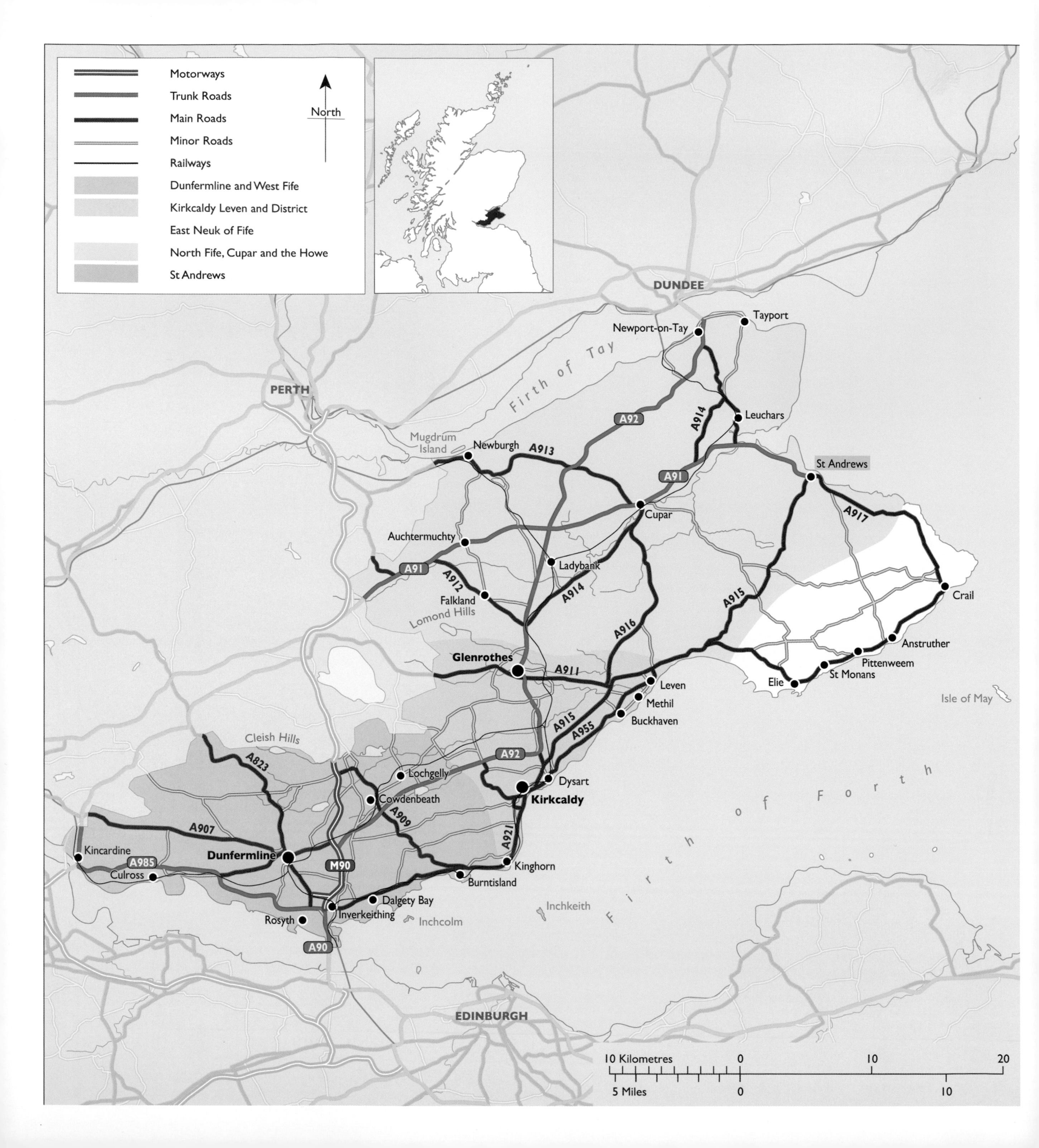
Motorways
Trunk Roads
Main Roads
Minor Roads
Railways
Dunfermline and West Fife
Kirkcaldy Leven and District
East Neuk of Fife
North Fife, Cupar and the Howe
St Andrews
North
DUNDEE
Tayport
Newport-on-Tay
Firth of Tay
PERTH
Leuchars
A914
A92
Mugdrum Island
Newburgh
A913
A91
St Andrews
Cupar
A917
Auchtermuchty
Ladybank
A91
A912
Falkland
A914
Crail
A915
Lomond Hills
A916
Anstruther
Glenrothes
Pittenweem
A911
St Monans
Elie
Leven
Methil
Isle of May
Buckhaven
A915
A955
Cleish Hills
A92
A823
Lochgelly
Dysart
Cowdenbeath
Kirkcaldy
Firth of Forth
A907
A909
A921
Kincardine
A985
Dunfermline
Culross
M90
Kinghorn
Burntisland
Dalgety Bay
Inchkeith
Rosyth
Inverkeithing
Inchcolm
A90
EDINBURGH
10 Kilometres
0
10
20
5 Miles
0
10

Alastair Campbell

Fife from Above

Deveron
Publications

For Alastair and Chloe from Grandpa

First published in 2011 by

Deveron Publications

Academy House,
Shedden Park Road,
Kelso TD5 7AL

ISBN: 978-0-9553110-2-4

British Library Cataloguing-in-Publication Data

A catalogue record of this book is available on request

Book and jacket designed by Mark Blackadder

Printed and bound in Singapore by Tien Wah Press Pte. Ltd.

Contents

Acknowledgements

The majority of photographs have been supplied by Aerial Photography Solutions, with a number captured specifically for this publication. My search for material also led me to the following main sources: National Library of Scotland (NLS); the archive of the Royal Commission on the Ancient and Historical Monuments of Scotland (RCAHMS); the Scottish Cultural Resource Archive Network (SCRAN); the collections of the National Monuments Record of Scotland (NMRS); University of St Andrews Library; and Fife Council.

A number of the communities are reflected through the Royal Air Force oblique aerial photographs, from the late 1940s, that are held at NMRS. Those images contributed to the Scottish part of the National Survey of Great Britain undertaken by the Royal Air Force, to support the Ordnance Survey with their map revision during the post-war years. An additional dimension to this book is the reproduction of 16th- and 17th-century maps of Fife. These record the work of cartographers John Geddy, father and son James and Robert Gordon, and the 19th-century map-maker John Wood. The engravings and drawings by John Slezer, in the late 17th century, have also been sourced from the National Library of Scotland's map department.

I am also most grateful to a number of people who have provided information, material and advice. They include Ann Belton, Andrew Beveridge, Lorna Campbell, Sheila Campbell, Janice Erskine, Neil Fraser, David Galloway, Guthrie Hutton, Isobel Kirk, Lesley-Anne Lettice, Jim Lewis, Bert McEwan, Jillian McFarlane, Margaret McNicol, Elsie NicIlleathain, Betty Pryde, Laragh Quinney, Frank Rankine (Methil Heritage Centre), Sandra Reid, Martin Rogers, Mairi Shiels, Elaine Shipp, Graham Turnbull, Kristina Watson, Ann Watters MBE, Ken Whitcombe, Jimmy Wilson, Johnston Wood and Elizabeth Young.

I am also indebted to David Edwards, proof-reader, Mairi Sutherland and to Mark Blackadder for his expertise in design of page and cover.

Finally, no one is more deserving of my gratitude than my wife Margaret as I strived to achieve the numerous deadlines.

Alastair Campbell

Introduction

The peninsula of Fife has to the north the Firth of Tay, to the east the North Sea, and to the south the Firth of Forth. The area has presented a fertile landscape for centuries, supporting one of Scotland's most intensively farmed regions. Fish, weaving and coal have also contributed to a strong economic base. Historic buildings and an industrial heritage reflect a rich vein of history. Through associations to local legend, the area, at times, is referred to as the 'Kingdom of Fife' or just 'the Kingdom'.

Dwellers have existed from the Mesolithic period through to the Bronze and Iron Ages. The first millennium AD saw Pictish tribes occupying lands north of the Forth, inclusive of Fife, known then as 'Fortrif' to the west of a line south of Auchtermuchty and 'Fib' or 'Fif' to the east, from which derives 'Fife'.

Historical landmarks are evident across the Kingdom, one of the most significant being Falkland's Royal Palace, a National Trust property in the shadow of the Lomond Hills. On the east coast is the Royal and Episcopal Burgh of St Andrews, founded in 1140, a superb planned medieval town and home to Scotland's oldest university. Numerous castle ruins around the coastline serve as a reminder of less peaceful times. To the west is Dunfermline, the former capital of Scotland, with its Abbot House, Royal Palace and ancient Abbey, the final resting place of kings and queens, including Robert the Bruce. The picturesque settlements of the East Neuk are major attractions, as is Culross to the west, with pantiled roofs, white-washed cottages and cobbled streets all restored to the grandeur of a 17th-century village.

Fife has also been synonymous with coal for centuries. After nationalisation in 1947, the coalfields reached their peak in 1967, employing 24,000 miners. Through the centuries mines have been worked, from the Clackmannanshire boundary in the west, through the southern half of the Kingdom to Buckhaven. Coal-mining activity also existed in the north-east but had concluded well before nationalisation. In the late 1940s, the largest concentration was around Cardenden, Cowdenbeath, Kelty and Lochgelly. However, the largest collieries were at Seafield, Michael and Wellesley, between Kirkcaldy and Methil. To the west, Blairhall, Comrie and Valleyfield were important, with of course the Longannet complex by the late 1990s becoming the largest producer of coal in Scotland. Since the 19th century, Fife coal has undoubtedly fuelled a complex, diverse industrial base. Coal has been crucial to the development of alumina, iron, lime-burning, linen, engineering, paper, jute, floorcloth and linoleum industries.

Distinguished residents of Fife, over the years, have impacted on the life of others across the world. Kirkcaldy, the largest town, is proud of being the birthplace of the distinguished economist Adam Smith and Sir Sandford Fleming, Chief Engineer on the construction of the Canadian Pacific Railway. Dunfermline continues to value its legacy, through the generosity of local man, the industrialist and philanthropist Andrew Carnegie.

Geographically, Fife is impressive, with 115 miles of coastline and 61 miles of landward boundary that encircle rolling hills commanding a patchwork landscape. The Cleish Hills are to the west, the North Fife Hills overlook the Firth of Tay, and the Lomonds roughly divide the Kingdom into west and east. Drainage patterns are attracted to the River Ore and River Leven as they flow towards the Firth of Forth, through Largo Bay. The River Eden also captures streams as it makes its way east to the North Sea at St Andrews.

Fife was a county of Scotland until 1975, before becoming a local government region with three districts, Dunfermline, Kirkcaldy and North East Fife, until 1996. Since then, the functions of the district councils have been exercised by the unitary Fife Council. Today, in the second decade of the 21st century, the population is over 360,000, almost a third of whom live in the three principal towns, Kirkcaldy, Dunfermline and Glenrothes. With improved internal communications, new industries continue to make a positive impact on the prosperity of those who choose to live or work between Forth and Tay.

An added dimension to this publication are identified links for some areas to audio recordings from communities archived by the Scottish School of Studies at Edinburgh University, BBC Scotland and the National Trust for Scotland, all contained within the online project *Tobar an Dualchais/Kist o Riches.*

Historically, the first view of Fife from above must be credited to Vincenzo Lunardi, an Italian balloonist whose first courageous aerial voyage in Scotland, on 5 October 1785, saw him successfully navigate his hot-air balloon from Edinburgh to Ceres. If only Lunardi could have captured that first aerial view! Alas there were no cameras then, only press reports.

Fife from Above presents a diverse archive of maps, engravings, audio recordings, ground and aerial photographs that encapsulate the craft of those who, for centuries, have recorded this special corner of Scotland. I hope you enjoy viewing, listening and reading about the communities and landscape that make up the Kingdom of Fife.

Alastair Campbell

Dunfermline and West Fife

Aberdour

This historical Firth of Forth village, opposite Inchcolm Island, has Edinburgh and Leith as a distant skyline. Meaning 'At the mouth of the Dour', Aberdour was once in two parts, Easter and Wester Aberdour. It was the natural harbour at the Dour Burn, along with the high headland, that encouraged the two villages to develop. Easter Aberdour became a burgh of regality in 1638 after Wester Aberdour was made a burgh of barony in 1501. The prosperity of the two villages was due to St Fillans Church, the Castle and the nearby Inchcolm Abbey. Early trading with the continent, especially the Low Countries, resulted in the construction of a stone pier in the 1700s, which was later extended. However, as neighbouring Burntisland improved its harbour facilities and the railway arrived in the 1890s, the commercial importance of Aberdour's harbour declined. Fortunately, Silver Sands became a major tourist attraction, with excursion paddle steamers from Leith and Newhaven sailing to and from the wooden pier at Hawkcraig Point, especially built to cope with low tides. The rail link to Edinburgh, after the opening of the Forth Rail Bridge in 1890, generated the development of substantial residential properties, for city commuters. Today the old stone pier is still valued by leisure craft and artists. The award-winning railway station still provides an important daily link to the capital.

Steamer at Hawkcraig Point c.1900

Aberdour Castle

Aberdour Castle was within the land of the Barony when in the early 14th century Robert the Bruce granted the land to his nephew, the Earl of Murray. As time passed, this land was owned by the Douglas family, who became the Earls of Morton, one of the most powerful families in Scotland in the late Middle Ages. On suffering fire damage in the early 18th century, the Castle was abandoned as the Morton family's main residence, in favour of Aberdour House. However, it was not until 1924 that ownership was passed to the care of the Secretary of State. Today the Castle is in the care of Historic Scotland.

St Fillan's Parish Church

St Fillan's Parish Church is a striking memorial to St Fillan, an 8th-century Irish saint who became abbot of St Andrews.The present parish church has at its core a building dating from around 1140, consisting of a nave and small chancel, constructed in the Romanesque style. Around 1500, a Gothic south aisle was added along with a south porch soon after. Further major alterations took place in 1588 with a burial aisle added on the north side in 1608. However, in the late 1780s a new church was built in the main street and served as the place of worship until 1927. The medieval church, then a ruin, was restored in 1925–26. The new roof of thick Angus stone slabs reflected the same profile as the 1588 one and provides a generous sweep down to the low wall on the south side.

Aberdour looking east 2011

Right. Aberdour Castle and St Fillan's Parish Church 2011

Below. Aberdour Silver Sands with Hawkcraig Point 2011

Binnend Village

North of Burntisland once stood Binnend village, comprising two parts, High Binn and Low Binn. High Binn was built on the Whinniehall Estate. In 1891 there were around 135 houses at High Binn, and a population of around 600. Low Binn had around 30 houses with a population of about 190. This community was the result of the establishment of the Binnend shale mine and oil works in 1878. The oil works closed in 1893. The houses had a bedroom and kitchen with an outside toilet. Former resident Jimmy Wilson moved from West Linton to High Binn with his family in 1922, when he was seven years old, leaving High Binn in 1934. He can recall the shop, the school and the hall. However, the absence of basic facilities and improved local housing resulted in the formal closure of the villages around 1931. It was not until 1954 that the last inhabitant departed. Little of the village remains.

High and Low Binn 2011. The area in the foreground, with ruins of buildings, was the site of High Binn. The man-made pond is part of the drainage scheme as a consequence of waste from the aluminium complex. Within the wooded area top right, to the left of the small rectangular filtration pond, was Low Binn. Burntisland Golf Course is to the right.

High Binn

Early morning at the Binn c.1920

Binn village c.1923

Low Binn

The Low Binn c.1930

Burntisland

Burntisland, a coastal town between Aberdour and Kinghorn, became a Royal Burgh in 1541. As a major naval base in the mid 16th century it also had sea mills that used tidal power to saw timber and mill grain, which operated for three centuries. Ferries plied to and from Newhaven from the 16th century.

It was at St Columba's Church, Burntisland, in 1601, when King James VI attended the General Assembly of the Church of Scotland, that a proposal was put forward for a new translation of the Bible into English. The original printing of the King James Version was published in 1611, and used for 350 years as the Authorized, or King James, version.

By the mid 17th century Burntisland was chiefly engaged in exporting coal. Reaching their peak in 1800, the herring fleets frequently offloaded their catch to supply the eight curing factories near the harbour. Prosperity was evident through the local coal industry, and the arrival in 1848 of the Edinburgh and Northern Railway opened up the Burntisland to Kirkcaldy and Cupar line. The harbour was the terminal for the new Granton steam ferry in 1850, the world's first train ferry. It was also a fishing port of registry with the code BU, supported by coopers, net-makers, gutters, packers and vendors.

As the 19th century progressed, the volume of coal exports increased, resulting in the construction of six coal hoists in 1901. The completion of the Forth Rail Bridge, eleven years earlier in 1890, resulted in the extension of the rail track to Inverkeithing to cross the Forth. The train ferry service consequently ceased but the passenger service continued until 1940, with a brief reintroduction from 1949 until 1952, and then a catamaran for a year in 1991.

The North British Aluminium Co. bought ground in Burntisland in 1913 although it was 1917 before the first imports of bauxite arrived for conversion into alumina. After a merger with Canadian firm Alcan in 1984, the plant finally closed in 2002. Wilfred and Amos Ayre from Tyneside began shipbuilding in 1918, a major industry, until the final vessel, *Helen Miller*, was launched in 1969. In the early 1970s, part of the former shipyard site was used for the construction of service modules for North Sea oil-rigs, an activity that continued, with peaks and troughs, into the 21st century. Burntisland is a popular holiday destination, and has a population of over 5,000.

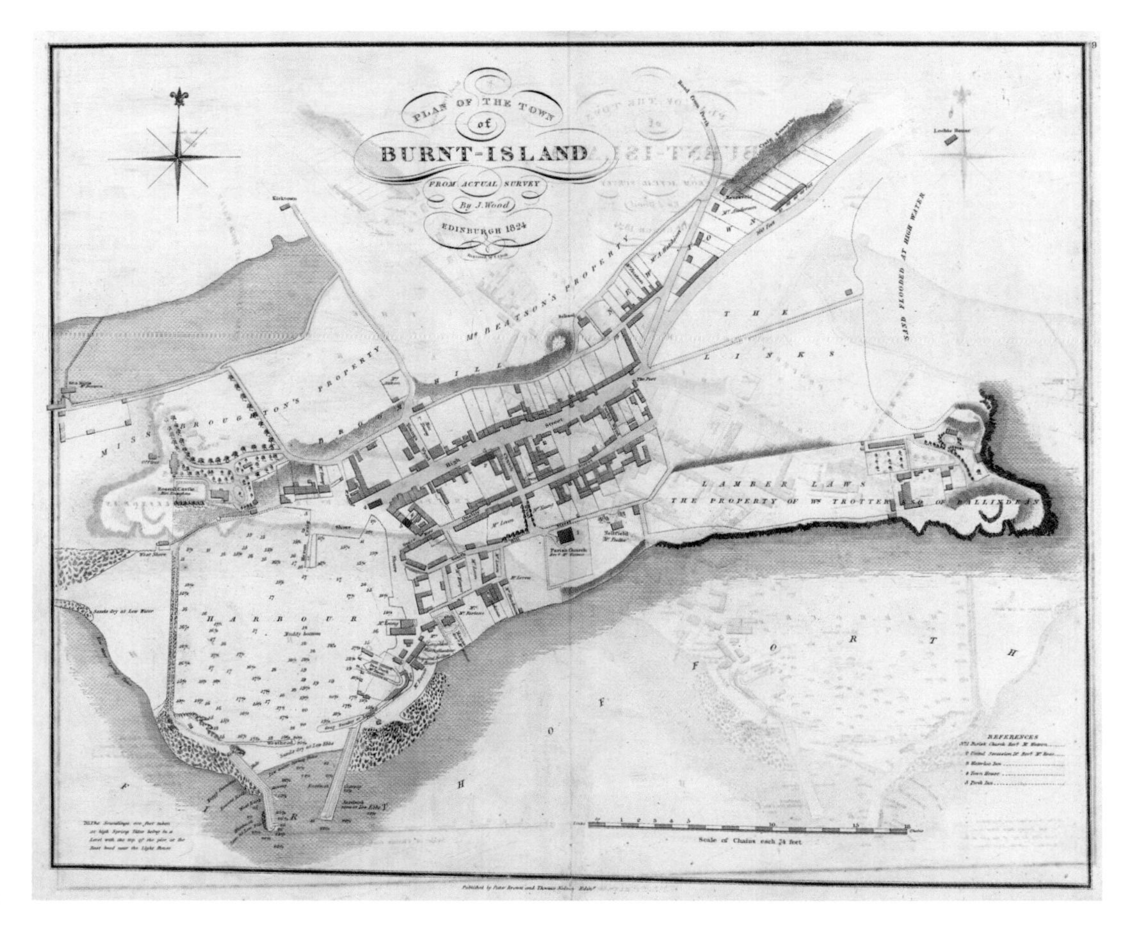

Map of Burntisland by John Wood 1824

Burntisland, May 1948

A Shipyard
B Oilcake Mill
C Sea Mill
D Aluminium Works
E The Barns
F Episcopal Church
G Palais de Dance
H Gas Works
I Picture House
J Railway Works
K Police Station
L Loco Coaling Shed
M Slaughter House
N Hydraulic Engine Shed and Tower
O Dock

Aluminium works after closure 2003

Housing development on site of former aluminium works 2011

Charlestown

Charlestown is on the north shore of the Firth of Forth between Culross and Rosyth. It was a model village created by Charles, 5th Earl of Elgin (1732–1771), to house labourers for his limeworks. He built kilns, six initially, the number eventually growing to fourteen. He laid out a harbour from which coal and quicklime was carried to the rest of Scotland. The village was set out in the shape of its founder's initials, CE, with terraces of harled houses, pantiled and slated, the simplest of designs built first in Double Row, with the more distinctive in North Row, c.1820. This shoreside community was once one of the most important industrial centres in Scotland. Prior to the impact of coal extraction and lime conversion, there was an established iron industry making use of locally quarried ironstone. Production of lime diminished from the 1930s, with the limekilns closing in 1956. Since 1990, restoration work has been undertaken. Today the original concept of the community can still be appreciated.

Charlestown with the limekilns overlooking the harbour 2010

Cowdenbeath

Five miles east of Dunfermline lies Cowdenbeath, a community that originated around 1820. By 1827 there was a small group of houses, and the Old Inn had been built at the junction of the new turnpike road to Burntisland. The search for iron ore unearthed coal seams, which resulted in the opening of a coal mine in 1844. A rail link, the Dunfermline branch of the Edinburgh & Northern Railway, later the North British, opened from Thornton in 1849 with a station close to the Old Inn. From 1852, Lumphinnans No. 1 pit was sunk for ironstone, but it was the coal seams that proved to be more lucrative. The result was the rapid growth of Cowdenbeath into a town with a population of 2,700 in 1881, and the establishment of a junction for the rail link to Kinross. By 1888 Cowdenbeath was a large town, with new-build housing very much dependent on the adjacent collieries. By 1894 it was called 'a colliery centre', with mineral railways and nine coal-pit shafts being operated by the Cowdenbeath Coal Company: Lumphinnans Nos. 1, 2, 7 and 11; Cowdenbeath Nos. 3, 7 and 9; Fulford No. 1; and the 394 ft deep Mossbeath pit. By 1896 the Fife Coal Company had taken these over. Close by was the Newton Colliery, and east of the town the Arthur and Foulford pits, with the latter also producing 20,000 bricks per day in the 1890s at its large brickworks. South of Foulford, the Gordon Colliery was worked from 1893.

1895 saw the start of the Fife School of Mining, which finally closed in 1976. Trams arrived in 1909, when the Dunfermline Tramways Co. constructed an electrified line linking Dunfermline, Crossgates, Hill of Beath, Cowdenbeath, Lochgelly, and later Lochore. The population of Cowdenbeath in 1911 was 14,000. Cowdenbeath Football Club was formed in 1905, and by 1917 Central Park was its home pitch, next to No. 7 pit. The town's population continued to expand. The Miners' Institute in Broad Street was built between 1925 and 1928. However, the coal strike of 1926 devastated the community. The Kelty tramline closed in 1931 due to subsidence, and the remainder of the tramway ceased in 1937. The Gordon pit closed in 1939, with Mossbeath continuing until 1945; the old Lumphinnans No. 1 pit closed in 1957. Cowdenbeath Colliery closed in 1960. Ten years later the Perth and Kinross railway closed, but a passenger service continued to Dunfermline and Edinburgh.

In the 1970s, employment gained momentum. A new clothing factory and a large double-glazing factory were established. Shell Expro built the massive NGL fractionation plant at nearby Mossmorran. In the early 1990s a third fractionation plant was constructed, followed by another module in 1994. Today Cowdenbeath High Street reflects the shopping patterns of the 21st century, with evidence of a drift towards shopping malls in nearby towns and the closure of long-established trading outlets.

Cowdenbeath 1960

A Mine Rescue
B Baptist Church
C Broadstreet School
D Moss Side School
E Central Park
F West Church
G Co-op
H NCB Workshops
I Abatoir
J Cairns Church
K Thistleford Farm
L Thistle Public House
M Rail Wash Houses

Above. New houses at the north end of the town 2011

Left. The High Street travels from the centre towards the top right corner 2011

Cowdenbeath from the south looking north; the A92 can be seen top right 2011

Sir James Black (1924–2010)

James Black was a miner's son who moved from Uddingston to Cowdenbeath in his early years. He attended Beath High School before gaining a scholarship to St Andrews University to study Medicine. While teaching in universities at home and abroad he also worked for major drug companies; this culminated in the development of the beta-blocker, a life-saving drug which has revolutionised the treatment of heart problems. He also developed a stomach ulcer drug called cimetidine. He was appointed to the Order of Merit, the highest honour bestowed by the Queen, and is only the second Scot ever to have won a Nobel Prize for Medicine.

Culross

The village of Culross, pronounced coo-russ, is 12 miles west of the north end of the Forth Bridge. It was at this Royal Burgh, according to legend, that the King of Lothian's exiled daughter was washed ashore in the 6th century. The early religious community was founded by St Serf, the mother of St Kentigern (or St Mungo), who in turn founded his own religious site in what is now Glasgow. St Mungo is Glasgow's patron saint. His birthplace, St Mungo's Chapel, now in ruins, lies to the east of Culross.

Coal mining was started by the Cistercian monks of Culross Abbey, and in 1575 the unique Moat Pit was built, with a mine shaft being driven beneath the sea bed to be linked to a man-made island (Preston Island) from where coal was loaded onto ships. Preston Island still has remains of coal mines and salt pans. James VI granted a Royal Charter in 1588, authorising coal exports. The harbour, called Sandhaven, then saw the export of coal and salt to the Baltic states and the Low Countries. The returning ships had as ballast red pantiles, many of which still roof the town's houses. This lucrative trade benefited Sir George Bruce, owner of the salt pans and coal mines. He built Culross Palace as his home between 1597 and 1611. His elder brother Edward built the Abbey House in 1608. The Mercat Cross, dating from 1588, and the Tron, where export cargoes were weighed, were essential to the Burgh's trade. The Town House, built in 1627, the centre of local government for many years, dominates Sandhaven. This former prison for debtors has a clock tower that was added in 1783. Today, the Royal Burgh of Culross is without doubt the finest and most complete example of a 17th- and 18th-century Scottish town, the result of excellent conservation work by the National Trust for Scotland since 1945.

John Slezer's *The Prospect of ye House & Town of Colross* 1693. It was a group of rocks in the river Forth that provided John Slezer with a vantage point to capture this prospect of Culross. The rocks were easily accessible at low tide. The figures in the foreground give a distorted idea of the size of the rocks: they are actually quite small. The Abbey ruins and surviving church dominate the skyline, with Culross House and its extensive gardens to the right.

Culross Abbey House

Culross Abbey House was originally built in 1608 by Edward Bruce, elder brother of Sir George Bruce. Unroofed in the early 19th century, the main block was repaired in 1830 by Sir Robert Preston of Valleyfield. It was remodelled by Robert Hurd & Partners in 1954–56.

Overleaf. Culross village with the Abbey and Abbey House visible top right 2011

Culross Abbey

To the north of the community is the ruined Culross Abbey, founded in 1217 by Malcolm, Earl of Fife, as a small Cistercian monastery with monks from Kinloss Abbey in Moray. The Abbey church was restored in 1633. The eastern parts of the Abbey church are the present parish church.

Culross Abbey and House 1973

Admiral Lord Thomas Alexander Cochrane (1775–1860)

Scotland's greatest naval hero, Thomas Cochrane, is buried in Westminster Abbey. He is honoured in Fife by a plaque at Anstruther, in the name HMS Cochrane, the former shore base at Rosyth, and most recently by the placing of a bust outside Culross Town House. Born at Annfield near Hamilton, the son of 9th Earl of Dundonald, Cochrane spent much of his early life in Culross, where his family had an estate. A sea career as a senior British naval officer during the Napoleonic Wars was combined with election to the House of Commons and a reputation as a radical Member at Westminster. However, Cochrane's unpredictability, combined with a highly inventive mind and remorseless valour, saw him dismissed from the Royal Navy in 1814. He continued his sea exploits as Admiral of the Chilean, Peruvian and Brazilian navies. Subsequent service also saw him Commander-in-Chief of the Greek Navy. He succeeded to his father's title, as the 10th Earl of Dundonald, in 1831, and to a seat in the House of Lords. A change of government, and a change of heart towards Cochrane, saw him reinstated with an Admiralship in the Royal Navy.

Cochrane's bust and Town House 2010

Overlooking the village green and Sandhaven is Culross Palace with its distinctive orange walls 2011

Culross Palace

Although it was never a royal residence, Sir George Bruce's home was visited by King James VI in 1617. The property today reflects a unique restoration of a merchant's town house, with kitchen gardens growing plants that link back to the 17th century.

Dalgety Bay

The coastal, privately built, New Town of Dalgety Bay lies to the east of the Forth Bridges and functions as a dormitory suburb of Edinburgh and other Fife towns. It has been developed since the early 1960s on a site that is thought to date back to a 13th-century village. Coal exports and salt production merited the building of St David's Harbour in 1752. Despite this investment, by the early 19th century the coal and salt trade had declined, resulting in buildings being demolished. The population moved away, and the hamlet became a lost village. Today's community commenced with the first new houses in 1965, months after the opening of the Forth Road Bridge. Due largely to the resulting road link to the capital, the town has expanded considerably, as has the local Donibristle Industrial Estate. The unstaffed railway station opened in the late 1990s, linking the community to the main east-coast line. A large national supermarket and garden centre are now established, enhancing the town's facilities for its 10,000 residents.

Below. St David's Harbour (man-made) in 2011 reflects a different scene from a ship-breaking yard in the 1950s

Opposite. Dalgety Bay with the Donibristle Industrial Estate at top of photograph 2011

St Bridget's Kirk

The remains of this Kirk, with origins dating back 850 years, can be seen just above the shoreline to the east of Dalgety Bay. The rebuild of the original church was consecrated in 1244 by David de Bernham, the Bishop of St Andrews, and dedicated to St Bridget (or Brigid) of Kildare in Ireland, who lived from 451 to 525. St Bridget's was altered in the 17th century, only to become unsafe in the early 1800s when the roof collapsed. A keep can be seen within the churchyard walls, a viewing point to guard against body-snatchers! The Kirk remains are maintained by Historic Scotland.

St Bridget's Kirk 2011

Dunfermline

Dunfermline is Fife's second largest town, 5 miles inland from the Firth of Forth and to the west of the M90 route north. This City and Royal Burgh, once the ancient capital of Scotland, is thought to have been a significant settlement as far back as the Bronze Age. The location of a fortified tower within Pittencrieff Glen is thought to reflect its name, 'fortress by the crooked stream'.

Around 1060, King Malcolm III, Malcolm Canmore, selected the town as the site for his new royal residence. Queen Margaret, his second wife, arranged for the building of a monastery for Benedictine monks, on the site of the nave of the present abbey. Both Malcolm and Margaret died in 1093. Margaret's son, David I, decided to re-establish his mother's priory as a full abbey. It was her burial place and he intended it to become the dynastic mausoleum of the Scottish Royal House. Dunfermline Abbey was founded in 1128, bringing additional Benedictine monks from Canterbury. It was completed in 1250, similar in layout and detail to Durham Cathedral. Only the nave of the medieval church survives but it is still one of the finest examples of Scoto-Norman monastic architecture. A chapel to St Margaret was added in 1250 when she was canonised for her faith and strong links with the church in Rome. The Abbey and shrine to Saint Margaret were renowned across Europe. This impacted on Dunfermline being the centre of monastic life and the court for almost 500 years.

The body of Robert the Bruce was buried at the Abbey in 1329. At his request his heart was taken on a crusade by Sir James 'the black' Douglas. Douglas was killed in a fight against the Moors in Spain. The embalmed heart of Robert the Bruce was returned to Scotland and is thought to have been interred at Melrose Abbey.

In 1620 parts of the vault of the south aisle were rebuilt, followed by the strengthening of the

John Slezer's *The Prospect of ye Town & Abby of Dumfermling* 1693. This view of Dunfermline was taken from the ruins of Malcolm Canmore's tower to the west of the Abbey, and shows the remains of the Abbey Church and the ruins of the Palace buildings.

aisle walls of the nave with heavy buttresses, a major external feature. The 17th and 18th centuries witnessed major damage and a state of ruin, resulting in total collapse. The south-west tower was rebuilt in 1810. Today the east end is referred to as Church of Scotland Abbey New Church, rebuilt 1818–21. The Bruce Memorial Window, designed by Gordon Webster, is in the north transept and was installed in 1974, on the 700th anniversary of Bruce's birth. The lower centre panel, showing Bruce, also features the famous spider! The west end of this magnificent building is retained as an ancient monument, in the care of Historic Scotland.

The Royal Palace dates from the 13th century, the birthplace of David II in 1324, James I, of Scotland in 1394, and Charles, later Charles I, in 1600 and his sister Elizabeth, offspring of James VI/I. However, after the Union of the Crowns of Scotland and England in 1603, James VI and his court moved to London and the Palace fell into ruin. It too is now under the guardianship of Historic Scotland.

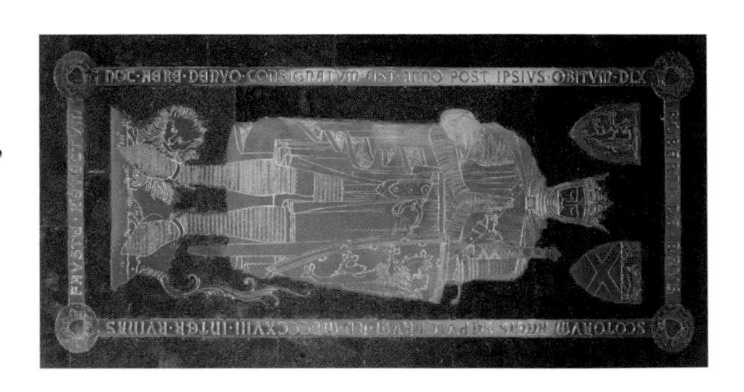

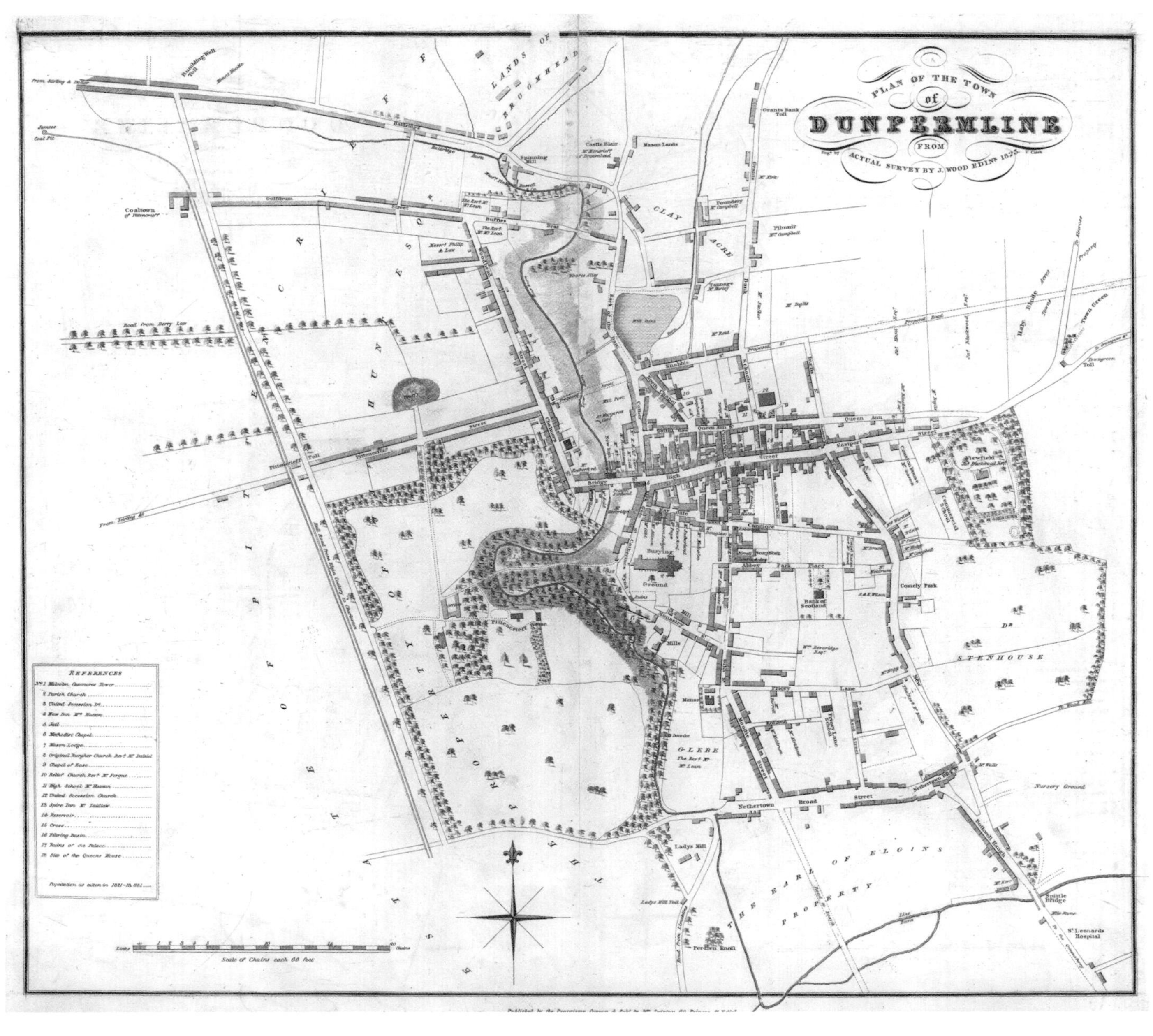

Above. The tomb of King Robert the Bruce, beneath the pulpit of Dunfermline Abbey Church. This commemorative brass plaque, embedded in marble, was the gift of the Earl of Elgin, a descendant of the king.

Left. John Wood's map of Dunfermline 1823

After a period of decline, Dunfermline began to thrive with the rise of the weaving industry in the 1700s. Access to the Forth ports and plentiful water saw damask weaving becoming established by the 1770s.

By the early 19th century, weaving was a well-established traditional industry. The east of Scotland climate was particularly suited to the spinning and weaving of linen, which was produced from locally grown flax. The weaving of damask was introduced in 1718 following the legendary story of James Blake who stole the secret from the weavers of Drumsheugh in Edinburgh by acting the 'daft laddie'. The early 1830s saw weaving as the dominant occupation in and around the town, with over 3,500 handlooms in operation in 1836. Over half of these were weaving damask, following the introduction of the'Jacquard' punched card system in 1825. Most of the weaving was carried out on handlooms in the weavers' houses, under contract from a merchant such as Mr Erskine Beveridge. To improve efficiency, handlooms began to be installed in groups in a weaving shed, and so the beginnings of the factory system evolved. In 1834 Beveridge retired from the drapery trade to devote himself exclusively to damask weaving, believing that if he promoted quality and good design he could succeed where others had failed. His taste in patterns was fastidious and he spared no expense in procuring the best designs. More than a hundred Erskine Beveridge damasks were shown at the Great Exhibition at Crystal Palace in 1851.

St Leonard's Works: Erskine Beveridge & Co. is acknowledged as the first of the successful power-weaving factories, opened in 1851. By 1869, St Leonard's was producing nine million metres of cloth per annum, with a turnover of £300,000, around a third of Dunfermline's total production. The handloom was virtually wiped out by the supremacy of the mechanical factory system. We can gain an insight into Mr Beveridge's success at St Leonard's Works from this contemporary account:

> At present there are four power-loom establishments in operation in Dunfermline, and others are in the course of erection. Erskine Beveridge & Co., St Leonard's Works, employ 709 powerlooms, which are driven by steam engines of 210 horsepower with 220 handlooms in the factory and more than this number outside; the number of hands being employed by this respectable firm being about 1500.
>
> A.J. Warden *Linen Trade, Ancient and Modern* (1864)

It was into this environment that Andrew Carnegie, the famous son of a handloom weaver, was born.

Above. Dunfermline Abbey and Palace 2008

Dunfermline, looking south, July 1947

A St Leonards Works
B Gas Works
C Dunfermline High School
D Rubber Works
E Cattle Market
F Regal Cinema
G Rosyth

Dunfermline, looking east, July 1947

A St Margaret's Works, Foundry Street
B Victoria Works, Pilmuir Street
C Pilmuir Works, Pilmuir Street
D Albany Works, Gardiner Street
E Fire Station
F Bus Station
G Opera House, closed 1955, demolished 1982, with the decorative plasterwork sold to the Asolo Centre for the Performing Arts in Sarasota, Florida, USA
H Carnegie Baths
I Pilmuir Hall, first Carnegie Baths
J St Andrews/Erskine Church
K Castleblair Works, Mill Street
L Canmore Works

Andrew Carnegie

Andrew Carnegie, Scotland's most renowned philanthropist, was born in 1835 at a small cottage in Moodie Street, now the Andrew Carnegie Birthplace Museum.

Along with his family he emigrated to the United States in 1848 and settled in Allegheny, Pennsylvania. He started work as a bobbin boy in a cotton mill, and later became a telegraph messenger boy. The Pennsylvania Railroad Company employed him as a secretary/telegraph operator from 1853, and his promotion was rapid owing to his astute business acumen. Carnegie invested in railroad-related industries: iron, bridges and rails. These slowly accumulated capital and became the basis for his later success. By 1864 he also had interests in oil wells. The demand for iron products, armour for gunboats, cannon, shells and many other industrial products contributed to him working with others to establish a steel-rolling mill at Pittsburgh, a centre for major steel manufacturing and the source of his fortune. After the American Civil War, Carnegie left the railroads to concentrate on ironworks. Earlier in his career he had noticed the weaknesses of the massive number of traditional wooden bridge structures on the railroads. Carnegie grasped the opportunity to replace them with iron bridges, manufactured in his works.

Carnegie continued to amass millions of dollars while stating his intentions to use his wealth for the benefit of others. His generosity was soon evident in his home town. In 1879 he donated swimming baths. He gave $40,000 for the establishment of a free library in Dunfermline, opened in 1883, the first of 2,509 Carnegie-funded libraries in the English-speaking world. In 1903 he founded the Carnegie Dunfermline Trust and bought Pittencrieff Estate for the town's folk, now called Pittencrieff Park. Carnegie continued to provide capital for purposes of public interest and the enrichment of educational advancement. He purchased Skibo Castle in Sutherland, along with a home in New York. His generosity towards his home town continued until his death at Lenox, Massachusetts, on 11 August 1919, aged 83 years. Carnegie was a philanthropist whose legacy is appreciated in Dunfermline and across the globe.

Central Library 1906. The world's first Carnegie Library. Andrew Carnegie's mother, Margaret, laid the library's memorial stone on July 1881. Two years later, in 1883, the library was officially opened by Lord Rosebery, later to become British Prime Minister.

Above. Weaver's Cottage 2010. Andrew Carnegie's birthplace on 25 November 1835. The family lived in one room. Another family lived in the adjoining cottage. The adjacent Memorial Hall was added in 1928. This is now the Andrew Carnegie Birthplace Museum.

Right. Andrew Carnegie as Rector of St Andrews University (1901–07), artist H.R. Butler

Dunfermline, looking west with the the A907 at top of photograph 1965

A Public Park
B Lower Station
C Aberdour Road
D Abbey View Housing Estate
E Woodmill Road
F Linburn Road
G Broomhead Flats

A Victoria Works
B St Margaret's Works
C Canmore Works
D Pilmuir Works
E Upper Station
F Albany Works
G Engine Sheds
H Coal Hopper
I East End Park (DAFC)
J Council Works, former jail
K Castleblair Works

Dunfermline, looking west from East End Park 1965

By 1989 the last of the Erskine Beveridge & Co. linen works had closed down, industry had begun to diversify to include electronics and oil-related companies, based on the expanding, edge-of-town industrial estates. Shopping centres occupied central locations as the housing base expanded dramatically. Dunfermline is now a community with a historic heart, which has developed to accommodate the commercial, social and industrial demands of the 21st century, all within thirty minutes of Scotland's present-day capital.

South and south-east Dunfermline 2010. In the foreground are Calais Muir Wood and Mid Duloch where water features, centre, reflect the sustainable urban drainage scheme.

Above. North and east Dunfermline from Halbeath 2010

Right. Cental area Dunfermline, looking east to East End Park at top of photograph 2007

Forth Rail Bridge

Traversing a natural narrow on the Firth of Forth between North and South Queensferry, this was the first major steel bridge in the world. The globally important cantilever structure, 1½ miles in length, was constructed between 1883 and 1890 and designed by Sir John Fowler and Sir Benjamin Baker.

Right. Forth Rail Bridge 2009

Below. The Forth Bridges 2005

Forth Road Bridge 2009

Forth Road Bridge

West of the Railway Bridge, the Forth Road Bridge, opened in 1964, has the distinction of being the largest suspension bridge in Europe at that time. Including the approach viaducts, it is over 1½ miles long. The main towers extend to 512 ft above the mean river level, with a central span of over 3,300 ft; the dual roadways and cycle paths are suspended from high-tensile steel wires within a cable 2 ft in diameter. Mott, Hay and Anderson, along with Freeman Fox and Partners, led by Sir Gilbert Roberts and William Brown, designed the structure. Sir William Arrol & Co. built the bridge at a cost of £11.5 million.

High Valleyfield

A former mining village midway between Dunfermline and Kincardine, High Valleyfield is situated on an escarpment, above Low Valleyfield, on the coast of the Firth of Forth. The village was built in 1941 after Valleyfield House was demolished on part of the Valleyfield Estate.

High Valleyfield 1976

Inverkeithing

Inverkeithing lies 5 miles south-east of Dunfermline, on the Forth shore at the mouth of the Keithing Burn (hence the name). In the early 1100s it was a trading port, and by 1153 it had become a Royal Burgh and one of the ports for Dunfermline. A number of religious buildings existed before the Reformation, including a Franciscan friary, Greyfriars, probably founded in 1268 by Philip de Mowbray. There was also a Dominican monastery. The church tower dates from the 14th century, as does the Hospitium of the Grey Friars, now the local museum. The medieval mercat cross is a rare survivor. By 1322, Inverkeithing was the main Scottish port for English trade. A tidal port, its main trade was in wool. By the late 16th century, coal was mined at nearby Fordell, with exports through Inverkeithing starting in 1683. The pier was extended in 1738 and table linens manufactured from 1744. By 1783, the wooden Halbeath Wagonway connected the harbour to the mines at Halbeath. In 1827 the Boreland distillery was built just to the north, with the addition of large maltings in the mid 19th century. Shipyards were in operation by 1869. A tunnel was driven under the town's eastern side, to permit the station to become a mainline junction when the Forth Rail Bridge opened in 1890. In 1921 Thos. W. Ward started large-scale ship-breaking that included World War II battleships, cruisers, and even aircraft carriers. In 1965 the Cunard liner RMS *Mauretania,* over 35,000 tons, was dismantled here (see photograph below).

During the 1980s and 1990s, electronic firms set up and then moved on. Paper making continued through the 1980s into the 1990s, employing over 200 people. Ship-breaking also continued to operate on a smaller scale. A major 'park and ride' was completed at Jamestown in 2000, to encourage commuters to leave their cars in Fife and travel by train to Edinburgh. Today Inverkeithing is almost continuous with Dalgety Bay and Rosyth.

Inverkeithing 1965

Inverkeithing 2006

Inverkeithing railway station, centre of photograph 2010

Kelty

Kelty lies 2 miles north of Lochgelly, close to Lochore Country Meadows Park. In the 18th century it was a small, nucleated settlement on the old North Road. It was at Kelty where the Fife Coal Co. was formed in 1872, impacting greatly on the lives of West Fife miners, through the acquisition of Hill of Beath (1887), Cowdenbeath (1896), Lochore and Capledrae (1900), Blairadam (1901) and Bowhill (1909). 1910 saw the Dunfermline tramways extended from Cowdenbeath, as a single track to Kelty. However, colliery subsidence affected the tramlines, resulting in the Kelty line closing in 1931. After World War II, Aitken power station employed over 1,200 workers, Lumphinnans complex employed nearly 800, and the Lindsay complex around the same number. By the late 1950s employment started to decline. The Benarty mine closed in 1959, Blairenbathie in 1962, the Aitken in 1963, the Lindsay in 1965 and Lumphinnans Nos. 11 and 12 (Peewit) in 1966. By 1991, the population was under 6,000. This former mining village now serves as a commuting base for those who wish to benefit from the close proximity of the M90 motorway.

Kelty, looking east April 1949

A Aitken Colliery and Power Station
B Lumphinnans Nos.11 and 12 (Peewit)
C Lindsay Pit

A Kelty Bus Station
B Oakfield Church
C Bowling Green
D Regal Picture House
E Blackhall Square

Kelty, looking east to west along Station Road and Cocklaw Street 1966

Left. Kelty east, showing more housing developments, and former surface buildings of the Lindsay Pit within the square area (lorry park) lower right, 2011

Below. The M90 heads north, with Kelty and Loch Leven separated by Benarty Hill on which the Fife boundary line runs eastwards, towards Navitie Hill, to drop south beyond Ballingry (out of photograph), 2011

Top. Kincardine with the Scottish Police College to the rear of the town 2011. Devilla Forest, stretching to back right, is composed chiefly of Scots pine and has an extensive network of paths and forest roads.

Above. Scottish Police College at Tulliallan Castle 2011

Kincardine

Kincardine on Forth, at the western end of the Kingdom, was created a burgh of barony in 1663. A pier was constructed around 1740 and small ships were built. In the 1780s coal was exported in exchange for flax, iron, wood, linseed and barley. The West Port brewery was built in 1798. In the early 1800s Kincardine was linked by ferry to the Falkirk area at Higgins Neuk close to Airth. When local government was reorganised in 1890, it appeared strange that the village became part of Fife and not Clackmannanshire. In 1936 the ferry was replaced by a road bridge. Coal was being mined in 1939 at nearby Castlehill. By the early 1950s the village had a population of over 2,000; the Scottish Police College at Tulliallan Castle started training courses in 1954. In 2008 a new bridge crossing was opened to the west of the 1930s structure, part of a new road system that reduces traffic volume within the community.

Kincardine Bridges

This first road bridge, foreground, was opened in 1936, with a steel centre span, the longest swinging span in Europe at that time. This permitted ships to sail up river to both Stirling and Alloa. When construction commenced in 1932, Willie McGregor was both Bridge Master and Harbour Master. Today the bridge has Category A listed status by Historic Scotland. The new bridge to the rear, seen under construction, was opened in 2008 and has the name *Clackmannanshire Bridge*. The site of the demolished Kincardine Power Station is on the right between the bridges. The Fife boundary approaches the Forth up river from the new bridge.

Kincardine Bridges 2008. In the foreground the first road bridge, and beyond it the most recent Kincardine road bridge, across the Forth

Kincardine Power Station

Kincardine power station, a 375 megawatt coal-fired power station, occupied a site west of Kincardine on the Fife–Clackmannanshire boundary. The interim British Electricity Authority started constructing the low-grade coal power station in 1952, burning 6,000 tonnes per day. This facility, with twin towers, began operations in 1962 and was demolished in 2001.

Kincardine power station 1967

Knockhill

Opened in 1974, 5 miles north of Dunfermline, Knockhill Racing Circuit is Scotland's National Motorsport centre. Ongoing developments, both with the track and motorsport facilities, have resulted in this corner of Fife playing host to most of the major British car and motorcycling championships. This image is taken from the eastern end of the circuit.

Right. Knockhill Racing Circuit 2008

Limekilns

The community at Limekilns dates back to the 14th century when it was a fishing village with a natural harbour, serving as the main port for Dunfermline. In the early days, limestone was important for farming improvements and for mortar. Industry soon developed using kilns fuelled by charcoal, and later coal, to convert lime to quicklime. From 1750 the industry moved the mile to Charlestown where massive industrial-scale limekilns operated until 1956. In its lifetime this picturesque village has been home to a number of industries, including shipbuilding, soap making and brewing. To the rear of the village is Broomhill House, on land once owned by the monastery of Dunfermline. This is the seat of the Earls of Elgin and Kincardine. Housing estates developed in the 1970s and 1980s.

Above. Limekilns 2010

Lochgelly

Situated east of Cowdenbeath and Lumphinnans, a village existed at Lochgelly by the late 18th century. A lease for mineral rights was granted by 1836 to a company which became the Lochgelly Iron Company in 1851, and then the Lochgelly Iron & Coal Company in 1872. Coal was the main mineral from the 1870s. The 1849 opening of the Edinburgh & Northern Railway's Thornton and Dunfermline branch, on which Lochgelly's station was built, was significant. Lumphinnans No. 1 Colliery was sunk in 1852. The Nellie pit was sunk in 1880, as part of the Lochgelly Colliery. The Rosewell Colliery was sunk around 1884. By 1909 the Dunfermline Tramways Company linked Lochgelly via Cowdenbeath. In 1912 the tramway was extended to Lochore, but the whole system closed in 1937. The Jenny Gray pit was closed in 1959, and the Nellie Colliery had closed by 1965. The Nelly site was reclaimed from 1967 for part of the Lochore Meadows Country Park. All main mineral workings collapsed before the early 1970s, apart from some opencast activity. The Fife bus garage closed in the early 1980s.

Lochgelly was also associated with the infamous 'tawse'. Around 1885, Robert Philip, a saddler and ironmonger, was the first to produce the leather strap which some teachers used to enforce painful corporal punishment on culprits within many of Scotland's classrooms. Thankfully all local authority schools had abolished the strap by 1987.

Lochgelly 1947

A 'Pre-fabs'
B East School
C Railway
D Alexander's Bus Garage
E Happy Land
F Jenny Gray Pit
G Roman Catholic Chapel
H Co-op Bakehouse
I Neilson Bakehouse
J Town House
K Picture House

Main Street looking west, Lochgelly c.1911

A South Primary School
B Library
C Co-op
D Miner's Welfare
E North School
F Convent
G St Patrick's School
H Town Hall
I Water Tower
J Opera House
K Berry Street Flats
L West Primary School
M Slaughter House
N Fire Station

Lochgelly 1966

Station Road, Lochgelly c.1911

Lumphinnans in the foreground with Lochgelly behind, looking east, 2011

Main Street (centre) Lochgelly, heading east, 2011

Auchterderran, Bowhill, Cardenden and Dundonald

In the foreground Auchterderran, Bowhill with cemetery in the centre, Cardenden top left and Dundonald top centre, 2011

Cardenden

Coal mining is thought to have started here as early as the 15th century. A branch of the Edinburgh & Northern Railway was constructed in 1848 from Thornton Junction to Dunfermline, with Denend the only colliery at that time. A station was built and named Cardenden by the rail company, close to Bowhill Bridge, south of Auchterderran. The village gradually developed and in the 1920s and 1930s its expansion was linked to increased mining activities. The local Corrie Centre is named after the local poet Joe Corrie (1894–1968), once described by T. S. Elliot as 'the greatest Scots poet since Burns'. John Thomson (1909–31), known as the 'prince of goalkeepers', played for Celtic against Rangers in 1931 when, after a freak collision and resulting head injury, he died. Reports indicate that over 30,000 attended his funeral at Bowhill Cemetery. Cardenden is also the birthplace of bestselling crime author Ian Rankin (1960). Dundonald, Bowhill and Auchterderran are all within the immediate area.

Cardenden (centre foreground), Dundonald (top left), Bowhill and Auchterderran (top right) 2011

Dundonald

Dundonald 2011

A small community close to Cardenden

Crosshill, Lochore and Ballingry

LOCHORE

Lochore is a former mining village that takes its name from the nearby Loch Ore. It is linked to Ballingry village to the north and Crosshill to the south.

Above. Crosshill in the foreground, Lochore (centre) and Ballingry (rear) 2011

Left. Lochore in the foreground with Ballingry to the rear 1965

Lochore Meadows Country Park

This reclaimed coal-mining wasteland, north of Lochgelly and south of Loch Leven, was host to a number of pit-heads, including the Mary pit, whose winding gear structure dominates the park as a monument to the area's mining legacy. Within the park's 1,200 acres is Loch Ore, 260 acres, which has facilities for boating and fishing. The three islands are named Tod, Whaup and Moss. The meadows, grasslands, ponds, woodlands, nature reserve and a nine-hole golf course are open to all who wish to explore and enjoy the great outdoors.

Right. Outdoor Education Centre and Park Centre at east end of Loch Ore 2011

Below. Lochore Meadows Country Park, looking west 2011

Longannet 2008

Longannet Power Station

On the upper Firth of Forth, east of Kincardine, the giant 2,600 megawatt coal-fired station at Longannet has foundations of 270,000 m^3 of concrete and a 1,600 ft chimney stack that dominates the skyline. River water is used as a coolant, rather than cooling towers. Construction began in 1962 and the complex was commissioned in 1972. The power station is operated by Scottish Power, part of a multi-national utility group; the main supply of coal is now sourced from opencast mines. In 2009 Longannet became the first UK power station to have a linked carbon-capture unit commissioned. This additional unit is planned to help moderate climate change, by storing the greenhouse gas, carbon dioxide, underground.

Mossmorran and Braefoot Bay Terminal

Mossmorran

The Mossmorran natural gas liquids fractionating plant processes gas from the Brent Fields and the Goldeneye Gas Platform. Located south of Cowdenbeath, the complex has been developed since the mid 1980s. The distillation process produces ethane, propane, butane and natural gasoline. The bright flare is clearly visible, day and night, from points north and south of the Firth of Forth.

Mossmorran 2011

Braefoot Bay Marine Gas Terminal

Between Dalgety Bay and Aberdour, Braefoot Bay is a tanker terminal for the export of liquefied petroleum gas from the nearby Mossmorran fractionating plant. It is operated jointly by Shell Expro and Exxon Mobil.

Braefoot 2010

Top. A bridge painter's view 1988

Above. Ferryboat *Sir William Wallace* 1952

North Queensferry

The village of North Queensferry sits on the north shore of the Firth of Forth, between the Road and Rail Bridges. It is named after Queen (later Saint) Margaret, wife of King Malcolm Canmore. This early ferry port was an important landing point for pilgrims heading to St Andrews and Dunfermline. By the late 1790s, the ferry was an important link in the daily postal service over to Queensferry. The Town Pier was designed and built between 1810 and 1830 by the eminent Scottish engineer John Rennie. It served the Queensferry passage for many years, later to be extended by another well-known engineer, Thomas Telford. The first steam-powered ferry was in 1821, suitably named *Queen Margaret*, with future ferries also named after notable Scots. The Forth Rail Bridge was opened in 1890. The last ferries to ply the crossing were *Queen Margaret* (1934–64), *Robert the Bruce* (1934–64), *Mary Queen of Scots* (1934–64), *Sir William Wallace* (1956–64). The Forth Ferry service ceased to operate when the Forth Road Bridge opened in 1964. Situated east of the Rail Bridge, in the disused Battery Quarry, is the Deep Sea World aquarium, which also opened in 1964.

Above. North Queensferry 2002

Right. Invitation to opening of Rail Bridge 1890

Far right. North Queensferry Town Pier 2011

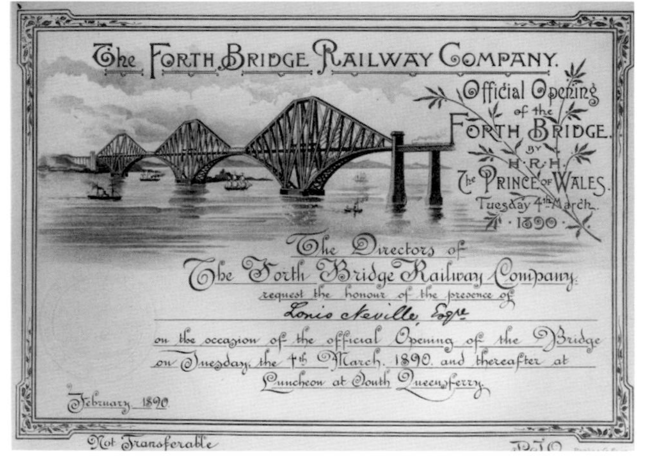

The Forth Bridge Railway Company.

Official Opening of the Forth Bridge by H.R.H. The Prince of Wales. Tuesday 4th March. 1890.

The Directors of The Forth Bridge Railway Company request the honour of the presence of Louis Neville, Esqre on the occasion of the official Opening of the Bridge on Tuesday, the 4th March, 1890, and thereafter at Luncheon at South Queensferry.

February 1890.

Not Transferable

P.T.O.

Preston Island

This former island has some of Scotland's most significant early-19th-century coal-mining remains, alongside well-preserved salt pans, all situated east of Culross. Having been surrounded by deposits of fly-ash from neighbouring Longannet Power Station, it is now effectively part of the mainland. Back in 1575, the coal mine was leased by Sir George Bruce and by 1604 he had constructed an artificial island, through which a shaft emerged from the undersea workings, permitting the shipment of coal by boat when tides were high. The presence of a steam-engine house confirms the extent to which, by the beginning of the 19th century, steam power had revolutionised coal mining. Drainage problems had hitherto severely restricted the depth and extent of mining. The introduction of Newcomen atmospheric engines from 1712 greatly enhanced the scale of potential mining operations. The photograph shows the village of High Valleyfield behind the former island.

Preston Island 2011

Rosyth

In 1903 the Admiralty bought 1,248 acres of land on the north shore of the Forth, 3 miles south of Dunfermline. The construction of the Royal Navy Dockyard began in 1909, with Rosyth planned as a 'Garden City' to house the workers. Submarines, known at that time as K-class craft, first arrived at Rosyth in 1917. Placed on a 'care and maintenance' basis between the wars, a large number of vessels of the German High Seas Fleet were broken up in the 1920s and 1930s. The base was re-activated in 1939 and, after withstanding closures and decommissioning, finally closed in 1996. It included HMS *Cochrane* as a Fleet Accommodation Centre and an Apprentice Training Establishment. In 1997, the Naval Dockyard was acquired by Babcock International, which made the facility the first privatised naval dockyard in Britain.The dockyard is known as MOD Caledonia.

Rosyth is separated from Inverkeithing by the A90, which then becomes the M90 towards Perth.

Above. Rosyth Naval Base c. 1920s

Below. Rosyth, looking west from A90, Admiralty intersection foreground right 2010

In 2001 HMS *Invincible* was in port for a refit while HMS *Ark Royal* was about to leave for sea trials, after the completion of a refit. The third of the Invinvible Class carriers is HMS *Illustrious*; it can be seen in the main basin in the May 2011 image. The Goliath crane dominates the basin while some of the pre-fabricated sections of the new Queen Elizabeth Class carrier are visible near the centre and close to the crane. HMS *Invincible* was decommissioned in 2005 while HMS *Ark Royal* was decommissioned in March 2011.

Above left. Rosyth dockyard and port 2010

Above. HMS *Ark Royal* in the entrance dock with HMS *Invincible* in the background 2001

Left. HMS *Illustrious* in port while her replacement HMS *Queen Elizabeth* is constructed on the quayside, May 2011

St Ninian's Opencast Site

Scottish Coal's opencast site, St Ninian's, west of Kelty and adjacent to the M90 Motorway, is massive. Loch Fitty is in the background along with Dunfermline and the River Forth, at the top of the photograph. To date over 5 million tonnes of coal have been extracted, with the possibility of another 4 million tonnes as the site develops. Progress with the 'Fife Earth' project is also evident. The Scottish Resources Group, whose mines are broadly located within Scotland's central belt, are working with landscape architect Charles Jencks on what is clearly an imaginative restoration design. By using the overburden, removed from above the coal seams, a sculptured landscape will be created reflecting the continents of the world and a loch in the shape of Scotland. The area will provide a public recreation and leisure facility. Loch Fitty, until recently a popular trout fishery, is scheduled to be drained to permit the opencast workings to extend across the entire area.

Above. St Ninian's opencast site 2010

Right. Clear strata, St Ninian's 2010. With the M90 behind the trees, the extraction process proceeds, out of sight of passers-by. The dark coal seams are clearly visible between the other strata in the exposed rock face.

Kirkcaldy and Leven District

Buckhaven

On Fife's coast, 5 miles north-east of Kirkcaldy, the community of Buckhaven merges with Methil and Leven. The locals sometimes refer to it as 'Buckhind' or 'Buckhine'. The natural fishing harbour had its first pier built in 1840, which was then enlarged by 1853. From the mid 1850s net factories had become established.

Coal mining was a major employer from the mid 1850s when Muiredge was acquired by Bowman & Co. Denbeath was sunk in 1872–75, with an additional shaft sunk in 1883–85 to work the Chemiss seam. Bowman & Co. meanwhile had also sunk the Rosie pit in 1880, between Buckhaven and East Wemyss. The Laird of Wemyss built his own rail link between Thornton and Buckhaven. By the late 1880s, many of Buckhaven's men had given up fishing in preference for work in the mines of Methil, Wemyss and Cameron. In the early 1900s, there were still 30 local fishing boats. After 1901, the Rosie pit was connected with the Wemyss Private Railway. In 1905, the Wemyss Coal Company took over the Bowman concern, making improvements at Denbeath, sinking a third shaft to enlarge it, and subsequently renaming the colliery Wellesley. From 1906 to 1932, the Wemyss & District Tramway Company linked Leven and Buckhaven with Gallatown. In 1905, the model village of Denbeath, built by Wemyss Coal Company, had over 200 houses, which attracted Lanarkshire miners to an enlarged colliery that opened in 1910. The miners' rows were named after rivers (e.g. Spey, Tweed, Forth) and ran diagonally, rather than parallel, to the building lines. This was a 'Garden City'. By this time a number of churches were well established. In 1869, the fisherfolk of Buckhaven bought the Episcopal Church, North Street, St Andrews, and proceeded to transport the building, stone by stone, by fishing boats, to Buckhaven. St Andrew's Church, shown in the photograph on page 55, is the rebuilt building.

Electricity arrived in 1911 with gas coming in 1913. The library was established in 1925. A new Cameron drift mine was created in 1934, on the site of the old Isabella pit. The Muiredge pit closed in 1938. Netmaking finished in 1945. Owing to the dumping of coal waste on the beaches, the harbour became silted up. Fishing ceased in the early 1950s, and by 1970 the harbour had been infilled. The Rosie pit closed in 1953 and the Wellesley Colliery closed in 1967 owing to its impending exhaustion, combined with intense foreign competition. The former Wemyss Private Railway track closed during 1966–70. Chemicals, knitwear and the manufacture of roof trusses have provided employment in more recent times.

Buckhaven 2011

Wellesley/Buckhaven and Denbeath, July 1948

A Wellesley Colliery, part of the Wemyss Coal Company
B Denbeath
C The Skating Rink
D Wemyss Brick Works, a common secondary industry associated with coal mining
E Michael Colliery
F Wemyss Private Railway
G White Swan Hotel

Buckhaven, May 1948

A Miners houses built by Bowman & Co., coal owners of Muiredge and the original Wellesley pit
B St David's Church
C St Andrew's Church
D Muiredge Church
E Primary School
F Muiredge Colliery
G Miners' Hostel
H Rosie Colliery
I Part of East Wemyss

Dysart

Dysart is situated east of Kirkcaldy; by 1330 coal mining was already in progress there. As well as a fishing industry at Dysart, salt too was produced locally, along with hides, many of which were exported to the Low Countries. By 1435, Dysart was a Sinclair burgh of barony and, like Cupar, its merchants were trading with Danzig by 1444. Coal shipments to Denmark were evident in 1507, so there must have been a good harbour. Trading increased with links to Hamburg and Bergen. Profits were reflected within the community: the 16th-century St Serf's great church and the second solid tolbooth provide evidence. A burgh school was founded in 1579. In 1671, the local mine went on fire, not for the first time, resulting in the burgh becoming bankrupt. One hundred years on, shipbuilding was introduced, with

John McDouall Stuart
(1815–1866)

Stuart was born in Dysart and emigrated to Adelaide, Australia, at the age of 23. In 1862 he was the first European explorer to cross Australia, from Adelaide to Van Diemen Gulf, on the north coast, and back again. His Stuart name lives on, in the mountain, Mount Stuart, in Central Australia and the 950-mile road, Stuart Highway, between Alice Springs and Darwin. This Dysart son is acknowledged as one of the greatest of Australian explorers.

Dysart with Kirkcaldy (east) in top third of photograph 1947

A Viewforth Junior Secondary School
B Peter Greig & Co. Ltd, Linen Manufacturer
C Bowling Green
D Railway Line
E Barony Church
F St Serf's Church
G Town Hall
H Dysart House
I St Serf's Tower
J Birthplace of John McDouall Stuart
K Normand Hall

Above. Frances Colliery 1980

Below. Former site of the Frances Colliery with headframe 2011

Overleaf. Dysart and harbour with east Kirkcaldy top left 2011

timber imported from Germany, and there was a steady increase in weaving to 130 handloom weavers in the 1770s. The late 18th century was boom time! Over 700 looms made cloth from Fife-spun yarns; over 100 miners produced around 20,000 tonnes of coal annually, a high percentage of which was exported to Holland and Scandinavia in exchange for timber. Coal, salt and linen were also exported, while pantiles, clay for local potteries, flax seed, wine and spirits were landed in this Fife port. A steam ferry plied to and from Leith from 1819. By 1839, over 2,000 looms were active in the wider parish, employing over 5,000 people, producing around 34 million metres of cloth annually. A carpet factory was also within this community.

When the Frances Colliery, known as the Dubby pit, was sunk east of the town around 1875, its pit-head was located on the cliff top. At the end of the 19th century the harbour was thriving, supported by shipbuilding and the opening of a ships' chandler. Electricity in 1911 permitted an immediate extension of the Kirkcaldy tramway system to Dykehead. The boatyard and the then unused dock closed in 1929. In 1930 Dysart was absorbed by Kirkcaldy burgh, and a year later the tramway closed. By 1978 the Frances Colliery employed around 600 workers but in 1984 a fire broke out, during the miner's final strike, forcing the whole complex to close. This action brought to an end the environmentally disastrous tipping of coal waste, which for so long had damaged the beaches of Dysart and Kirkcaldy. Surface buildings were eventually demolished with the exception of the headframe, which survives as a monument to the Fife coal industry. The Frances Minewater Pumping and Treatment Site reflects the iron-ore within the four tanks. Today Dysart harbour has recovered to provide shelter for small yachts and shellfish craft. Little evidence remains of former industries and trade.

East Wemyss

Situated on the coast, 5 miles north-east of Kirkcaldy, lies East Wemyss, with the ruins of MacDuff's Castle. The area is thought to have the most caves in Europe, with eleven caves documented. It is most noted as a former mining community; coal production was focused on the Michael Colliery when production commenced in 1895/1898. Michael Colliery became the largest producer of coal in Scotland, employing at its peak in 1967 over 3,350 miners. Whilst still the country's largest pit, and after massive investment, a disastrous fire broke out in September 1967, destroying the new reserves. 302 men escaped, nine were killed resulting in the premature closure of the colliery. **Sir Jimmy Shand, MBE, MA** (1908–2000), world-renowned Scottish country dance band leader, was born in East Wemyss but lived most of his life in Auchtermuchty. **George Moodie** (1829–1923) was also born in East Wemyss. After studying navigation at Dundee and while working for ship owner Jock Willis, he was asked to supervise the building of Willis' latest ship, the tea-clipper *Cutty Sark*. Moodie became her first captain. He retired to Methil in 1891 and founded the bowling club, to which he donated the 'red duster' flag from the *Cutty Sark*.

Above. Michael Colliery 1967

Below. East Wemyss and site of former Michael Colliery 2011

Glenrothes

A Development Corporation was set up in 1948 to secure the layout and development of Scotland's second New Town, Glenrothes, stretching from the lower slopes of the East Lomond, across the valley of the River Leven, to just north of Thornton, Fife.

The town's name, Rothes, comes from links with the north-east Scotland Earl of Rothes, family name Leslie. It was the Leslie family who owned much of the land. Glen was added to avoid confusion with Rothes in Moray and because the town lies in the Leven valley.

Back in the 1940s, coal was the catalyst for planned development. With many Lanarkshire pits in decline, new sources were sought in Fife. Amongst these was Rothes Colliery near Thornton, reserved in 1936 by Fife Coal Company. An extensive programme of bores confirmed large reserves. It was estimated that within an area of around 10 square miles there were about 120 million tonnes of workable coal, to last 100 years at a production rate of 500 tonnes a day. Plans were made to have the most modern colliery of its day, using the 'horizon' system of mining, with excellent facilities for the men, along with the largest railway marshalling yard in Europe. Production started on 10 June 1957 but sadly it was a false dawn. By November 1959 there was a reduction in the recruitment of miners due to the falling demand for coal. However, the demand for coal was not the only critical factor as the Rothes Colliery encountered insurmountable geological and drainage problems, closing in 1962 after only five years of operation. This hugely embarrassing failure saw the central planning objective vanish. All efforts were now focused towards Glasgow overspill and further industrial development.

Today, Glenrothes is at the heart of Fife, successful and vibrant with a large indoor shopping precinct. Planning and landscaping have created quality space throughout the town. A high percentage of jobs are in manufacturing and public administration, with traditional industries still evident. Leading independent employee-owned papermaker, Tullis Russell, celebrated its 200th anniversary in 2009. A Fife firm, Tullis Russell is one of the world's leading environmentally focused papermakers and one of the town's major employers.

A 'Silicon Glen' background continues to impact with a number of high-tech companies specialising in electronics and engineering. Greater diversity is now evident, with a broad range of employment opportunities that include the headquarters of Fife Council. Glenrothes is a New Town proud of its first six decades, despite having to reinvent its original focus. Fife's central heart, Glenrothes, is in good health, fit to meet the challenges of the 21st century!

Glenrothes town centre 1964

Right. Barnton Place, Newcastle Precinct, Glenrothes 2011

Below. Glenrothes, general view looking from west to east 2008. Glenrothes Golf Course, east area housing and Leslie beyond the former railway viaduct. West and East Lomond are visible at the top of the photograph.

Lomond Hills

The Lomond Hills dominate central and north-west Fife. The twin volcanic peaks began their formation in the Carboniferous Age, some 350 million years ago. West Lomond rises to 1,810 ft, and East Lomond is the smaller at 1,390 ft. Lead was worked and silver extracted on East Lomond in the 18th century.

Left. Glenrothes 2006

Below. Glenrothes 2008. The town centre with Tullis Russell (papermakers) extreme right and looking towards Cadham and Balfarg top right.

Kinghorn

The community of Kinghorn was chartered in 1165 by Malcolm IV, his only Royal Burgh creation, to be rechartered in 1284 or 1285. A small harbour with little shelter exported small quantities of wool during the first half of the 15th century. Ferry rights existed in the 1500s for crossings to the Lothians, from both Kinghorn and nearby Pettycur. The Pettycur ferry closed with the introduction of the steam train ferry from Burntisland to Granton in 1850. By 1865, John Key had established a shipbuilding yard and in 1868 he built the first 600-ton iron whaler for a Dundee firm. The late 1870s saw the building of ferries, two of which plied the Burntisland to Granton crossing until 1937. The yard closed in 1909 to be reopened in 1919, and after the launch of the last ship, the SS *Kinghorn,* the gates were finally locked in 1921. By 1965 an inshore lifeboat station had been established. United Glass Containers opened a bottle plant in 1972, which closed in 1982. At the end of the first decade of the 21st century this village with a population of over 3,000 is now predominantly residential, accessed by road and rail.

Kinghorn divided by the main east-coast railway 2011

Above. Pettycur Bay Holiday Park, west of Kinghorn 2011

Left. Monument to Alexander III c.1910

Alexander III Monument

This memorial was erected in 1886 on a site overlooking Pettycur Bay Sands, near Kinghorn. Close to this spot in 1286, King Alexander's horse stumbled in the dark, throwing him to his death, down the 150 ft escarpment, thus bringing to an abrupt end the Golden Age of peace and prosperity in Scotland. Alexander III was the last of Scotland's Celtic kings. The Maid of Norway, his heir, died within four years, leaving a nation in turmoil, and with thirteen claimants to the throne, amongst them Robert Bruce and John Balliol.

Kirkcaldy

Fife's largest town, with a population of around 50,000, incorporated the former burghs of Pathhead, Linktown, Gallatown and Sinclairtown into the Royal Burgh of Kirkcaldy in 1876. The town acquired Dysart in 1930. Kirkcaldy is nicknamed the 'Lang Toun' because of its main street of just under one mile, recorded on 16th-century maps. The original area of Kirkcaldy existed as a burgh of regality by c.1320, dependent on Dunfermline Abbey. It was not until 1644 that Kirkcaldy was granted a formal Charter as a Royal Burgh, but it had been admitted to the Convention of Royal Burghs in 1574 and to Parliament in 1585. By the 1690s, the town was one of Scotland's top five ports. By the 1720s, great quantities of linen and corn were exported. At this time there were coal pits at the west end of the town close to the sea, and salt pans at the east end, along with a yard for building and repairing ships. Into the early 1730s the district, including the village of Leslie and the shoreside community of Dysart, was producing 170,000 yards of linen, annually. By 1800, close on a million yards of ticking (mattress covers) and other linen was woven annually in the town. By 1817, around 5,000 people worked in the local flax and linen industry. In 1822, James Aytoun built the first of three mills to spin tow, and in 1832 he began to spin jute. Whaling came to Kirkcaldy in 1816, peaking in 1828 with nine vessels. The fleet declined to five in 1834 and had disappeared by 1865. This was due to town gas replacing whale oil in lighting, both nationally and locally.

The Edinburgh & Northern Railway arrived in 1847, the same year that Michael Nairn built at the east end of the town an 'extensive establishment',

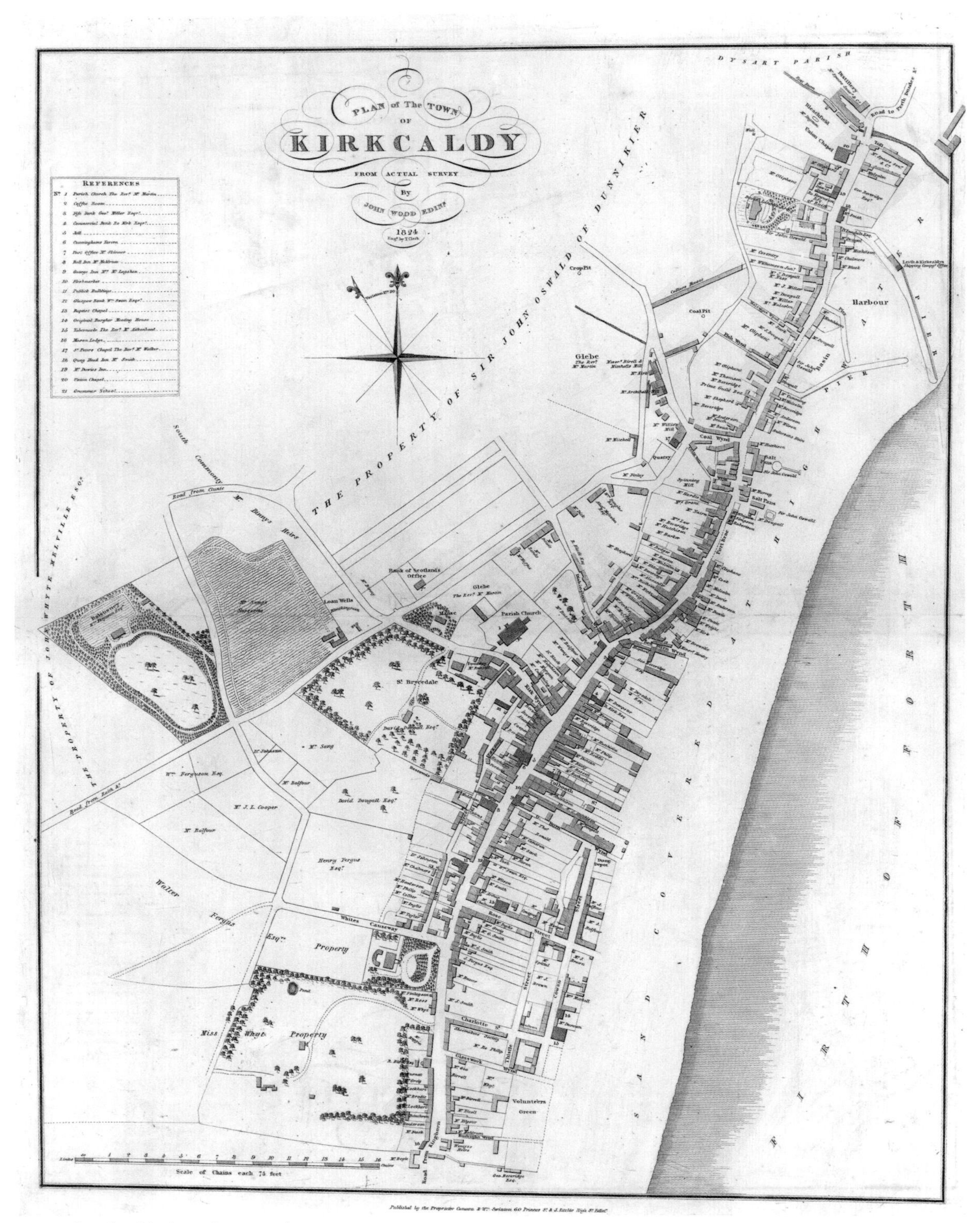

Map of Kirkcaldy by John Wood 1824

A Barry, Ostlere & Shepherd
B Abbotshall Church
C Bennochy Mill
D Baptist Church
E Foundations of Town House
F West End Congregational Church
G Railway Station

Kirkcaldy July 1947

having started canvas weaving south of Coal Wynd in 1828. His new factory made floorcloth (painted linen) and dominated the trade by 1862. Meanwhile the making of soft ropes began. In 1896, the Forth & Clyde Roperie made hard fibre ropes. N. & L. Lockhart built a factory in the mid 1860s and became the second largest fishing-net manufacturers in Scotland. By the late 19th century the town had developed into a carpet-weaving centre, with the Caledonian Linen Mills changing to Meikles' carpet factory. The Dunnikier Foundary, Douglas & Grant, John Key's Whitebank Foundry, James Brown, J.W. Mackie and the Tiel engineering works were all firms that contributed to Kirkcaldy's engineering output in the 19th century. A.H. McIntosh imported hardwood logs and opened the Victoria Cabinet Works in 1879. Raith Rovers eventually settled at Stark's Park in 1891–92, named after its owner, a local innkeeper and farmer.

The invention of linoleum is attributed to Englishman Frederick Walton. However, it was Michael Nairn who developed this special floorcloth, building on the patronage of the working class, who favoured 'lino'. Linoleum manufacture resulted in a distinct aroma, from the linseed oil, which impacted on all those who lived in and visited the town, until the industry's demise. The well-known poem 'The Boy in the Train' by M.C. Smith paints a vivid picture. The jute backing for the linoleum came from Dundee, the sawdust filling from Bo'ness, and the cork was imported from Portugal. Nairns continued to expand, while in 1899 a combination of other businesses and competitors merged to form Barry, Ostlere & Shepherd, whose factories were close to the railway station.

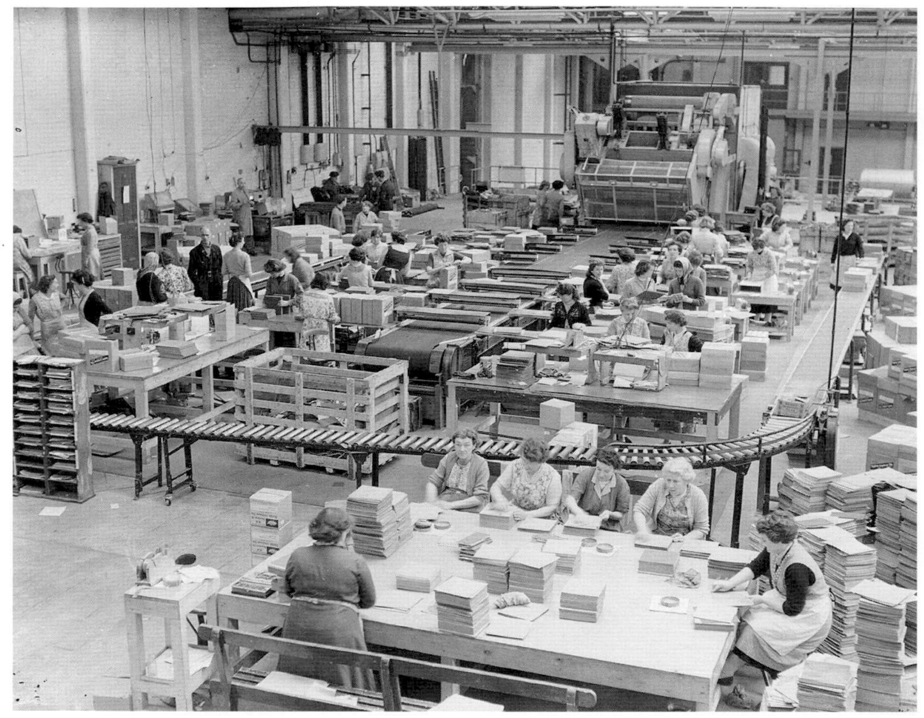

M. Nairn & Co. Linoleum Works 1954

Beveridge Park (1890–92) was a bequest from linen manufacturer Michael Beveridge. The Kings Theatre was built in 1904, later to be called the Hippodrome, by 1930 the Opera House, and from 1937 it became the Regal, the ABC, the Cannon and then again the ABC. Around 1908 the Palace Cinema was opened. Two of the other cinemas were the Rialto, which became the Gaumont, later the Odeon, in the High Street and the Raith in Link Street.

The single-line tramway opened in 1903, gauge 3 ft 6 in, and trundled from Linktown to Gallatown, through the High Street and via The Path. Another track provided an 'inland' route along Victoria Road, via the Victoria Viaduct to Gallatown. From 1906 Kirkcaldy had tram links to Leven.

As a way of relieving unemployment during the great trade depression, the Kirkcaldy Town Council built the sea wall in 1922–23. However, the placing of this barrier too far down the beach reduced the recreational use of this natural facility. The crowds did come but to the new Esplanade, where the annual April 'Links Market' was revived, soon becoming the largest street funfair in Europe, the spring gathering of the Scottish Showmen's Guild.

The tramways closed in 1931, three years after Walter Alexander had started buying out small bus companies which were trying to compete against the trams. Alexander built large garages on the Esplanade in the 1930s, converting the Tiel engineering works to a maintenance base.

The Boy in the Train
by Mary Campbell Smith

Whit wey does the engine say 'Toot-toot'?
Is it feart to gang in the tunnel?
Whit wey is the furnace no pit oot,
When the rain gangs doon the funnel?
What'll I hae for my tea the nicht?
A herrin', or maybe a haddie?
Has Gran'ma gotten electric licht?
Is the next stop Kirkcaddy?

There's a hoodie-craw on yon turnip-raw!
An' seagulls! – sax or seeven.
I'll no fa'oot o' the windae, Maw,
Its sneckit, as sure as I'm leevin'.
We're into the tunnel! We're a' in the dark!
But dinna be frichtit, Daddy,
We'll sune be comin' to Beveridge Park,
And the next stop's Kirkcaddy!

Is yon the mune I see in the sky?
It's awfu' wee an' curly,
See! there's a coo and a cauf ootbye,
An'a lassie pu'in a hurly!
He's chackit the tickets and gien them back,
Sae gie me my ain yin, Daddy.
Lift doon the bag frae the luggage rack,
For the next stop's Kirkcaddy!

There's a gey wheen boats at the harbour mou',
And eh! dae ya see the cruisers?
The cinnamon drop I was sookin' the noo,
Has tummelt an' stuck tae ma troosers.
I'll sune be ringin' ma Gran'ma's bell,
She'll cry, 'Come ben, my laddie',
For I ken mysel' by the queer-like smell
That the next stop's Kirkcaddy!

Kirk Wynd c.1910

Kirkcaldy 1969

A Barry, Ostlere & Shepherd
B Adam Smith Theatre
C Kirkcaldy Technical College
D St Bryceland Church
E Outer Harbour
F Inner Harbour
G Ravenscraig Castle
H Goods Depot
I Coal Marshalling Yard
J Hutchison's Flour Mill

Kirkcaldy 1966

A Gasworks
B Balwearie High School
C Forth View flat
D Burma Ballroom
E Beveridge Park
F Kirkcaldy Pottery site

Kirkcaldy looking east along the Esplanade 2011

From the mid 1950s to the mid 1970s the town became more of a service centre. New schools were built, including Balwearie Secondary School and Kirkcaldy High School. The Victoria Hospital and a largely new Forth Park maternity unit were completed. Established industries declined, and firms such as A.H. McIntosh, furniture manufacturers, moved to an industrial estate on the town's periphery. 1978 saw the former Technical College becoming the Fife College of Technology. The closure in the early 1980s of the town's last small iron and brass foundary, established in 1921 by John Leitch & Co., brought to an end the production of 'Kirkcaldy Pattern' manhole covers. Educational establishments continued to grow. In 1986 a new College of Nursing and Midwifery was opened, known since 1996 as the School of Nursing and Midwifery of Dundee University.

Kirkcaldy 1971

A Ravenscraig Castle
B Dunnikier Hotel
C Rio Cinema
D Dunnikier Estate
E Maltings
F Nairn's Factory
G Victoria Hospital
H Kirkcaldy High School
I General Hospital

The Mitchelston Industrial Estate 2011

Residential homes on the site of the former
Seafield Colliery surface buildings 2011

Kirkcaldy is a community that has a lasting legacy through its famous sons. It is the birthplace of the economist Adam Smith (1723–1790) and, five years later, the architect Robert Adam (1728–1792). Sir Sandford Fleming (1827–1915) lived in the town for his first seventeen years before emigrating to Canada. As an engineer, Fleming had responsibility for directing a series of surveys that mapped out the best route for the 2,000-mile-long Canadian Pacific Railway. He also proposed the introduction of a 24-hour international clock and suggested that there should be some form of Standard Time. His system is still in use today. He also designed Canada's first postage stamp, 'Threepenny Beaver'. Rt Hon. Gordon Brown MP, former Prime Minister and Leader of the Labour Party 2007–10, was born in Glasgow in 1951. When his father was called to be minister of St Brycedale Church, Kirkcaldy, Gordon attended Kirkcaldy West Primary School and Kirkcaldy High School before proceeding to Edinburgh University. He has been a Member of Parliament since 1983, first for Dunfermline East and currently for Kirkcaldy and Cowdenbeath.

At the beginning of the 21st century Kirkcaldy is no longer a major industrial centre but still has the oldest resilient floor covering manufacturer in the world, founded by Michael Nairn in 1847, now part of the Swiss-owned Forbo consortium. Good road and rail links enhance the commercial and retail activities. The Adam Smith Theatre contributes greatly to cultural life of the town. The Museum & Art Gallery, set in the town's War Memorial Gardens, hosts an outstanding collection of paintings that include what is probably the largest public collection of works by William McTaggart and Scottish Colourist S.J. Peploe outside the National Galleries of Scotland. The Glasgow Boys also feature, as well as works from Lowry, Sickert, Redpath and Bellany.

Kirkcaldy looking towards the Firth of Forth 2011

Wemyss Ware

The Fife Pottery, started by Robert Heron & Sons in the 1820s, produced creamware items and subsequently used the name Wemyss Ware from 1880s until the depression in the 1920s, when the company failed. The name was in honour of the family from the nearby Wemyss Castle. Limited production continued in Devon until the late 1950s. However, through direct employee links, stretching back to the final days in Kirkcaldy, the skills and techniques have been revived at the Wemyss Ware studio pottery in Ceres, resulting in the acquisition of the famous Trade Mark in 1994. Wemyss Ware has returned home to Fife. A superb collection of original pieces can be viewed within Kirkcaldy Museum.

Seafield Colliery

To the west of Kirkcaldy, the large Seafield Colliery was sunk south of Linktown and began production in 1967, to exploit undersea coals. It was later linked underground with Frances on the other side of Kirkcaldy. One of National Coal Board's most successful superpits, it operated for 22 years with an average workforce of 2,178. The miner's strike of 1984–85 saw the loss of two of the three coal faces. The pit finally closed in 1988, with the surface works being razed to the ground to make way for a housing estate.

Right. Seafield Colliery c.1975

Ravenscraig Castle

West of Dysart lies a castle that was planned before 1460 for Mary of Modena, the second wife of King James II. Despite King James being killed at the siege of Roxburgh Castle in 1460, building continued. Mary was in residence when she died in 1463. Ravenscraig was one of the first Scottish castles built with very thick walls to withstand cannon fire, and one of the earliest to have numerous gun ports designed for firing cannons. In 1470 King James III forced a swap with Kirkwall Castle, to gain the Earldom of Orkney, with Ravenscraig becoming the property of the Sinclair Earls of Roslin, based at Rosslyn Castle, who completed the construction. Despite being damaged by Oliver Cromwell's forces in 1651, the Castle remained a Sinclair possession until 1898. It was an ammunition store during World War I and is now maintained by Historic Scotland.

Ravenscraig Castle on the shore, within Kirkcaldy 2011

Leslie

Today, Leslie merges into Glenrothes, the dividing line being unclear. Fithkil and Fettykil were two previous names for Leslie. After the burgh of barony was chartered in 1458 it was named Leslie or Leslie Green after the Leslie family, Earls of Rothes in Moray. Spinning and weaving were at the heart of this community.

Leslie was a former centre for bull-baiting, with the Bull Stone still to be seen on the Green. Bulls were chained to this deeply grooved granite boulder to be baited by dogs. This sport was popular between the 12th and 19th centuries but declared illegal in 1835. Fettykil Mill, the original factory of Smith Anderson & Co. (1859–2006), was established by Charles Anderson, a local philanthropist widely recognised as an entrepreneur and inventor. 2010 saw papermaking return to the community, Sapphire Mill becoming established on the former Fettykil site. Today, the opportunities of nearby Glenrothes provide the places of work for many of Leslie's residents.

Top. Leslie Station, foreground extreme left, June 1947

Right. Leslie, looking east 2006

Leven

The 'Port of Markinch', 'Levynsmouth' at the mouth of the River Leven, had a harbour by 1435 and became a burgh of barony in 1609. The expansion of the town was linked to salt-panning, handloom weaving, fishing and eventually coal mining into the 20th century. In the early 1800s Kirkland Mill was making linen yarn from flax imported from Russia, and by 1810 it had the distinction of being the first mill in Scotland to be lit by gas. The harbour was expanded at this time to respond to increased trade. By 1836 there were five other spinning mills and about 170 weavers. A brewery existed by the late 1820s, as did a brick and tile works. An ochre (natural earth pigment) mine, a flint-grinding mill for pottery, and a sawmill were also working by the early 1830s. By 1867 there were a number of flax, hemp and jute mills, employing around 3,000 workers. Engineering was also well established in the 1860s with Henry Balfour

A Scoonie Parish Church
B Primary School
C Boas Spinning Mill
D Henry Balfour & Co. Ltd, Engineering Works
E Railway Line
F Gasworks
G Innerleven
H 'Bawbee Bridge'

Leven, looking east 1948

manufacturing vertical steam engines. Then, towards the end of the 19th century, winding engines for collieries, steel headgear and gasometers were manufactured. A new harbour was built in 1880. Unfortunately it did not match the superior coal-handling facilities at nearby Methil, resulting in closure by 1910.

George Nicoll, a young Leven blacksmith, in 1881 started making iron golf club heads, which led to the development of one of the best-known golf club manufacturers. Nicoll of Leven continued to manufacture sets of clubs, including woods, until 1983.

From 1904 to 1932 the electric trams of the Wemyss & District Tramway Company linked Durie Street in Leven to Methil, East Wemyss, Coaltown and Gallatown. As the adjacent Methil docks expanded, Leven docks were eventually infilled for the railway coal yard. In the early 1970s the giant DCL whisky blending and bottling plant, along with its many bonded stores, was developed at nearby Banbeath. In the late 1980s the town benefited from improved recreational facilities.

Above. West Sands Leven c.1905

Below. Leven, with bonded stores at Banbeath top left 2008

Markinch June 1947

Markinch

A small town, close to Glenrothes, Markinch was made a burgh of barony in 1673 and a police burgh in 1892.The classical Balbirnie House and its grand estate buildings were built in the late 1700s and early 1800s. Also in the early 1800s Robert Tullis & Co. of Cupar purchased the Auchmuty meal mill, south of Cadham on the River Leven. This was converted into a paper mill. Tullis also bought the Rothes paper mill in 1836 when steam power was introduced to both Tullis mills. Around this time, between Auchmuty and Sythrum there were twelve mills (paper, corn and weaving), along with bleachfields.

Balgonie and Balbirnie estates were both prosperous. It is to the Ballingall family that credit is given for local industrial development. Overseeing local coal mines, they also developed an excellent scheme to regulate the flow of the River Leven, from Loch Leven, for the great benefit of the riverside factories.

Markinch Station opened in 1847, generating more industrial prosperity, and a legacy of impressive public buildings and residential properties. The five-arch viaduct built with the railway is still a local feature. The former Haig's whisky bottling plant is now a buisness park. The railway station still provides an important link to both Dundee and Edinburgh.

Markinch, with former Haig's bottling plant in foreground 2011

Methil

At the mouth of the River Leven, the town of Methil was part of the former Burgh of Buckhaven and Methil and is within the urban area now known as Levenmouth, which also includes Leven. The village had salt pans in the 1500s and was a burgh of barony by 1662. Local coal was first exported from the tidal harbour in 1664. By the 20th century well over 1.5 million tonnes of coal had been exported, principally to Germany. By 1901 the new combined police burgh of Buckhaven and Methil was created. Coal exports continued to increase, with around 2.8 million tonnes by 1907. By 1910 passenger steamships plied between Leith and Methil. Aberhill brickworks opened in the early 1900s, and the Kirkland Steel Foundry was established in 1910, becoming the National Steel Foundry in 1914, to be extended in 1938. The tramway system closed in 1932, having opened back in 1906. Through to the 1950s much development was evident in a town that reached a population of around 13,000. Industry then began a downward spiral, with coal exports

Methil, May 1948

A Kirkland Coal Yard
B Kirkland Works, National Steel Foundary
C Methilhill
D Methil Docks
E Miner's Hostel
F Miner's Row

ceasing completely in 1976–77; Methil was the last coal port in Fife. In 1975 the burgh was brought into the new Kirkcaldy District. Between 1962 and 1966 a new 60 megawatt power station, designed to burn slurry from Coal Board washeries, was built at Innerleven, creating a landmark that has only recently been demolished. The oil boom of the 20th century impacted on this area of Fife in 1972, when the site of the former Wellesley Colliery was acquired by Redpath Dorman Long to construct massive steel-built oil platform jackets. Under Redpath de Groot Caledonian the yard went on to build a 9,500 tonne jacket for Total Dunbar, employing 750 workers from 1989 to 1992. Since 1951 Methil has been home to Jack Hoggan, a mining engineer who is better known today as the artist Jack Vettriano.

Methil 2011

East Neuk of Fife

Anstruther

Nine miles south-east of St Andrews, the East Neuk's largest town is a Royal Burgh, locally known as 'Ainster'. The coat of arms reflects three medieval burghs, Easter and Wester Anstruther, along with Kilrenny, all united since 1929. Included in this trio is Cellardyke, as the harbour for the burgh of Kilrenny; it was once called Nether Kilrenny. The boundary between Easter and Wester is the course of the Dreel Burn.

Anstruther gained its Royal Charter in 1587, permitting the holding of weekly markets and an annual fair.

In 1318 the monks of Balmerino Abbey, near Wormit, owned the land at Anstruther Easter harbour and leased areas to fishermen for the drying of nets. Rent was paid to the monks in salted herring. The popularity of herring remained, making Anstruther the capital of the Scottish herring industry in the 19th century, until the shoals declined during World War II. Through the centuries the impact of trade with Europe saw merchants bringing features of Dutch architecture to the town, such as curved gable fronts, which they incorporated into their own houses. Today, the harbour is a base for boats that catch shellfish, but the majority of boats are leisure craft benefiting from a sheltered marina and the pleasant waters of the East Neuk. Tourism is important, with the Scottish Fisheries Museum providing a unique insight into the Scottish fishing industry. The Fife Coastal Footpath and the Millennium Cycle Way also provide opportunities for those who wish to view the surrounding area at a leisurely pace.

Cellardyke

Most folk who stay in Kilrenny live in the area known as Cellardyke or Nether Kilrenny. Along with the two Anstruthers, the combined communities make one long town. The harbour, which existed by 1579, was called 'Skinfasthaven' on Gordon's Fife map (see endpaper). It was recorded as 'Siller Dyke' on Pont's map. Later it became known as Cellardyke. By the early 18th century Cellardyke had one street and a handful of fishing boats in a harbour that was largely rebuilt in 1829–31. In 1859, an oilskin, buoy and net factory was set up by Robert Wilson. A cod liver oil factory employed 20 people in the early 1860s and at this time local boat builders, Cunninghams, developed the straight-stemmed 'Fifie' hull form. In the early 1880s Cellardyke had the distinction of being Scotland's second most important fishing port, when over 200 boats were registered with the 'KY' Kirkcaldy registration. The great storm of 1898 devastated this Fife fishing community, with harbour piers wrecked and boats forced to use Anstruther. Today pleasure craft shelter in the harbour, and the village still reflects elements of a traditional East Neuk fishing community.

Opposite. Anstruther 2005

Below. Cellardyke 2006

Cambo

Between Kingsbarns and Crail is Cambo Estate. It is thought that the name Cambo originates from the fact that William the Lion granted lands to the de Cambhou family. In 1668 the estate was bought by Sir Charles Erskine and it is still in the Erskine family. The original mansion was destroyed by fire in 1878. Wardrop and Reid designed the present house in 1879–81, for Sir Thomas Erskine; it was later divided into flats in the late 1950s. Kingsbarns' old public clock is located within the tower. The surrounding grounds are open to the public over the summer months. 'Cambo' is now synonymous with 'snowdrops', with 300 varieties providing exceptional cover in the early Spring.

Cambo Country Park 2010

Crail

Crail was a Pictish fishing place, with a natural harbour. It was David I who chartered Crail as a Royal Burgh in the 12th century. He also built a castle that stood on the cliffs above the harbour, which fell into ruin in the 16th century. There is evidence of wool trade in 1427–31, which resumed in 1500–05. Prosperity was reflected through the building of the tollbooth in 1517, while the church became collegiate. By the 1690s the village exported over 2,000 barrels of fish annually. It had a Post Office by 1745, and five years later Roy's map recorded only one road coming south from St Andrews, the route that remains the main road today. Crail Golfing Society was founded in 1786. A tide mill operated by the 1790s. Lint was spun into yarn by hand, and local weavers made some 40,000 yards run of various cloths annually. With the harbour in poor condition, fishing declined from the late 19th century. The railway arrived in 1883 and became a catalyst for the development of Crail as a holiday destination. Into the 1930s the harbour was used for timber and potato imports. Burgh status was lost in 1975. With constrictions on private housing developments, Crail has managed to retain its attractive character, as an early Royal Burgh, supported by the National Trust for Scotland's 'Little Houses' restoration scheme. Today, artists and photographers capture images of a backdrop that includes small leisure craft, crabbing and lobster boats. It is perhaps the most photographed harbour in Scotland.

Above. Crail 2011

Crail Airfield

This area close to Fife Ness, the most easterly point of the Kingdom, was established as a military airfield during World War II. It was reactivated in 1940 to become a Royal Naval Air Base, HMS Jackdaw. By 1944 it was the base for No. 827 Squadron. By 1947 it had adopted the name HMS Bruce when it was a naval training establishment until closure in 1949. Subsequently it was an Army Transit Camp from 1950 to 1954 and the Joint Services School of Linguistics from 1955 to 1960.The site was then sold, with many buildings adapted for pig farming. Today, motorsport events make use of the former runways.

Right. Crail Harbour 2011

Below. Crail Airfield 2006

Elie and Earlsferry

Elie and Earlsferry are twin villages that were formally merged in 1930, surrounding a fine sandy bay, 8 miles east of Leven. Earlsferry's foundation is unknown because the original Royal Charter was destroyed by fire. A charter of 1589 granted the village free burgh status. Historians think that perhaps Malcolm Canmore did grant the village Royal Burgh status in the late 11th century, which would have encouraged trading links to the Low Countries and England. In 1498, along with Crail, Pittenweem and Anstruther, Earlsferry is recorded as one of the ports used by merchants trading with England. The name may be linked to the Earls of Fife who instituted a ferry that crossed the Firth of Forth to North Berwick, as part of the important pilgrims' route from the south to St Andrews. This came to an end with the Reformation in 1560, resulting in trade moving to the more suitable harbour at Elie in the late 16th century.

Elie at the eastern end of the bay built a church in 1639. A clock tower was added in 1729 when there were no buildings to the rear, hence there are only three faces! Coal had a significant impact over the

Above. A folly, east of the harbour, built as a summerhouse for Lady Janet Anstruther in the 18th century.

Below. Elie and Earlsferry, looking west 2002

centuries, probably starting around the 11th century, along with salt-making. Coal outcrops were accessed near the golf course and the west pier. Around 30 small coal pits existed in the late 18th century. Larger pits were sunk in the early 19th century, benefiting from steam-operated pumps and winding gear. However, a combination of difficult seams and miners becoming involved with fishing for herring resulted in mining ceasing around 1860. The Burgh had a number of cotton weavers until the 1840s when they converted to linen, using imported and locally grown flax. In 1863 a station was opened on the railway from Thornton Junction to Anstruther, encouraging the building of new houses and the renovation of older property, both for accommodation and shops. This new holiday destination, served in the 1880s by steamers from Leith, brought Edinburgh holidaymakers to the fine sands. The railway closed in 1964, impacting on the custom to local hotels. Elie is a community that still capitalises on its natural beauty, with pleasure craft and second homes contributing to the popularity of this East Neuk haven.

Elie 2005

Kincraig Point

Close to Earlsferry, Kincraig Point reflects a raised beach or marine terrace that has been raised above the shoreline by a relative fall in the sea level.

Top. Shell Bay

Right. This geological feature is on the shore adjacent to the Torrance Golf Course 2010

Fife Ness

Fife Ness is a vanished settlement where, in the early 19th century, stone was cut to shape, prior to the construction of the Stevenson Lighthouse on the North Carr Rocks, 1¾ miles off shore. There is evidence of a tide mill, a harbour and a kiln at this, the most easterly part of the Fife peninsula. Today there is the coastguard station and the Crail Golfing Society links, comprising Balcomie and Craighead Links. The Society is the seventh oldest golf club in the world, founded in 1786.

Fife Ness 2010

Kellie Castle

Three miles inland from Pittenweem, this Jacobean tower house dates from the 16th and early 17th centuries. It was owned by the Oliphant family from 1360 to 1613 and then bought by Sir James Erskine (1566–1639), a childhood friend of James VI who became Earl of Kellie. The tower house is the lower part of what is now the north-west tower. Further additions were made, reflecting a fine example of Scottish domestic architecture. The castle was abandoned for many years after the Earls of Kellie died. Professor James Lorimer and his family eventually rented the property from the Earl of Mar and Kellie, and began the restoration project. It was James' son, the architect Sir Robert Lorimer (1864–1929), who designed the gardens when just 16 years old. Continuing his father's restoration work, Robert restored the painted panelling and the grand plaster ceilings and designed furniture for the castle. Sir Robert's son, the sculptor Hew Lorimer (1907–1993), bought the castle in the late 1940s, together with the garden, and gifted the property to the National Trust for Scotland in 1970.

Top. Kellie Castle 2011

Above. Kellie Castle and gardens

Kilconquhar 2001

Kilconquhar

Two miles inland from Elie this village, pronounced locally as 'Kinucher', is joined to the neighbouring village of Barnyards. Kilconquhar Loch is overlooked by the parish church, built 1819–21, with its impressive 80 ft tower.

Kingsbarns conservation village 2010

Kingsbarns

This conservation village can be found 7 miles south-east of St Andrews on the A917 to Crail. It is thought that the name originated from the fact that barns in the area were used to store grain for the Royal Castle at Crail and the Palace at Falkland. Kingsbarns Golf Links, where the game has been played since 1793, is set in an amphitheatre along the coast, where most holes boast spectacular views of the North Sea.

Lower Largo

Adjacent to Lundin Links and overlooking Largo Bay, this small community was known as Largow Burnemouth in the 17th century. It was the birthplace in 1676 of Alexander Selkirk. The son of a shoemaker, Selkirk became a navigator, a voluntary castaway, and the probable model for one of fiction's most enduring characters. His story was romanticised by Daniel Defoe in *The Life and Strange Adventures of Robinson Crusoe of York, Mariner,* first published in 1719. A statue of Crusoe is on the site where Selkirk was born. A pier was built in 1827 and coal was exported. By 1838 a steam ferry plied across the Forth to Newhaven, connecting passengers to the Tay ferry and to Anstruther by horse-drawn buses. Over 30 herring boats were based here in 1855. The Cardy Net Manufactory, a fishing net factory, was built by David Gillies in 1867, employing over 25 women. This industrial building included a walled garden and a mansion for the owner, as can be seen from the illustration. This enterprise closed in the late 1950s. The railway arrived in 1857 and closed in 1966, having contributed to the development of the village as a recreational destination. Today the village is still popular, with many residents contributing to its affluent retired character.

Top. Cardy Net Manufactory, Lower Largo

Above. Robinson Crusoe statue in Lower Largo

Right. Lundin Links and Lower Largo looking east 2011

Lundin Links

This 19th-century village has now merged with Lower Largo. It is best known for its two golf courses, Lundin Golf Club, a pre-qualifying course for the Open Championship, and Lundin Ladies Golf Club, a nine-hole course. The second fairway of the ladies course has a cluster of three red sandstone standing stones, dating from the 2nd millennium BC.

Lundin Links 2011

Lundin Links foreground and centre, with Lundin Ladies Golf Club on the left. Lower Largo is in the distance.

Pittenweem

The name Pittenweem means 'place (pit) by or of the cave (weem)' and is of Pictish origin. The cave, where it is said St Fillan lived while he converted Picts to Christianity, is in Cove Wynd with the Saint's well and altar. However, the town's Patron Saint is St Adrian, who came from Hungary with his own group of Christian martyrs, only to be killed on the Isle of May in 872 during a raid by Danes. The town's coat of arms depicts St Adrian being rowed ashore from the Isle of May.

Pittenweem became a burgh of barony of its Augustinian priory in 1526 and a Royal Burgh in 1541. This resulted in the building of a harbour which was Scotland's main trade in cod and the second port for herring. As a burgh, weekly markets were held at which farmers sold their produce. Several annual fairs were also held. Shoes and linseed were sold on Lady Day, 25 March, wool at the Lammas Market in August, and cattle at the Martinmas Fair on 11 November. By the 1740s the main outer pier had been built, as had mills for grinding malt, indicating a local brewing industry. John Smith, clockmaker (1770–1814), made high-class clocks, a trade that was continued through to the 1850s by Smith's apprentice, George Lumsden, and his son.

Housing was the main development in the early 20th century. After World War II Pittenweem became Fife's premier fishing port, an accolade it still holds today. Further harbour developments took place in the mid 1990s. The fish-selling shed was replaced by a new fish market in 1994, to sell scallops, haddock, cod, whiting, prawns and lemon sole to merchants and fishmongers, many of whom have vans travelling to villages and towns across Scotland. The harbour continues to serve today's fishermen and hopefully future generations. Pittenweem is another gem on Fife's East Neuk, caring for the future, and proud of the many restored properties supported by the National Trust for Scotland.

Pittenweem 2011

Fife's principal fishing port, Pittenweem 2008

St Monans

Between Elie and Pittenweem, this East Neuk village had the name Inverin, 'the village at the mouth of the Inverie Burn or stream'. The present name reflects the presence of a shrine, said to contain the relics of St Monan, a missionary with St Adrian of May. Pilgrims were attracted to the shrine because of its healing powers, and as a consequence a community developed to provide food and shelter. It was to this shrine in 1346 that King David II came, according to legend, to receive successful treatment for injuries

sustained at the Battle of Neville's Cross. The Auld Kirk founded in 1265–67 by Alan Durward, Earl of Atholl, was built in its present form with the financial support of King David II. The magnificent church was damaged after the Reformation, and reroofed in 1646 to become the town's parish church. In 1828 additional restoration was completed under the guidance of architect William Burn. Further interior restoration was completed in 1955.

St Monans expanded after being chartered as a burgh of barony in 1596. During this period there were two distinct areas: an agricultural community on top of a raised beach, and the fishing village around the harbour. Despite exporting iron ore in the early 1600s, the port did not develop commercially. However, by the early 1700s there was a market, and James Millar & Sons timber boatyard was founded in 1747, a firm that closed in 1992. The St Philip's Saltworks were built in 1770s and used local coal until around 1825. The 18th-century windmill to the east of the town pumped water, used by the nine salt pans. Major harbour works in 1865 provided berths for close on 100 fishing boats. By the 1930s there were fewer than 40 boats and only 10 by the end of World War II. Today the Fife Coastal Path passes along the base of the protective wall sheltering St Monans Church, a striking and intriguing building commanding a superb location.

St Monans from the west, with the parish church in the foreground 2008

St Monans 2011

Upper Largo

Inland from Lower Largo, the nucleated settlement of Upper Largo was small in 1750. In 1792 linen was made for the British Linen Company by Pearson, and by the 1790s a number of local weavers made linen and checks. Extensive bleaching greens were well used. Central to the village is the 12th-century kirk, enlarged in 1688 and again in 1817. Sir Andrew Wood (c.1460–1539) is the village's most famous son, a medieval Admiral who was a merchant trader out of Leith. He has been referred to as the 'Scottish Nelson', as his ship *Yellow Carvel,* with 500 crew and 50 guns, defeated the English fleet in the Forth in 1498. Wood is the subject of the historical novel *The Admiral* by Nigel Tranter. The circular tower, foreground right in the photograph, formed part of the castle inhabited by Wood. The line of a canal, constructed from his mansion to the kirk at Upper Largo, is still evident. Wood was laid to rest at Largo kirk, but the year of his death is uncertain as no record can be found.

Upper Largo 2011

North Fife, Cupar and the Howe

Balmerino Abbey

Situated close to the Firth of Tay, 4 miles west of the Tay Rail Bridge in the small village of Balmerino, this Cistercian Abbey is thought to have been founded by Alexander II and his mother Ermengarde c.1227–29, by monks from Melrose Abbey. The church, dedicated to St Mary and St Edward, was built around the second quarter of the 13th century. A south aisle was added later, probably c.1286. The Abbey was destroyed by the English under the Earl of Hertford in 1547, with additional damage by Reformers in 1559. The Abbey is now under the stewardship of the National Trust for Scotland.

Balmerino Abbey, grounds and ruins 2011

Balmullo

West of Leuchars on the eastern slopes of Lucklaw Hill, this former weaving village is a popular dormitory community. In the early 20th century the cartoonist Martin Anderson lived in the area; his home was the red sandstone Cynicus Castle. He used the pseudonym 'Cynicus' when he produced satirical postcards from his factory at Tayport. Anderson died in 1932, and the castle was demolished in 1939.The quarry to the west of the village produces a red granite aggregate.

Balmullo 2011

Auchtermuchty 2011. The A90 from Milnathort to Cupar runs from the base of the photograph to the top right

Sir Jimmy Shand, MBE, MA (1908–2000)

World-renowned Scottish country dance band leader Jimmy Shand lived in the community of Auchtermuchty, having been born in East Wemyss. Shand was given the freedom of the Burgh of Auchtermuchty in 1974. The village proudly hosts a bronze sculpture of Shand, a memorial to the maestro's unique contribution to Scottish culture.

The Cross, Auchtermuchty c.1910

Auchtermuchty

On the A91 road between Milnathort and Cupar lies Auchtermuchty, known locally as 'Muchty'. A Royal Burgh since 1517, Auchtermuchty sits astride the Glassart Burn. It is a settlement that reflects its antiquity, with bridges, thatched roofs, stepped gables and red pantiles. Macduff House on the west side of the main square is the oldest house extant, dating from 1592. Employer John White commenced the manufacture of weighing machines in 1715, as the town was renowned for its grain trade and maltings. Linen dealers traded in the town by 1792, with imported flax arriving at Dundee and being brought to the local linen weavers. Linen weaving was a cottage industry that had 700 handloom weavers making linen in 1843. Peter Skinner's modern bleachfield employed 30 workers as late as 1864. The last loom ceased in 1912. After the collapse of a brewery company in the early 1800s, the Auchtermuchty distillery was established in 1829 by the Bonthrone family; it closed in 1926. The railway arrived in 1857 on the branch linking Kinross and Ladybank; it was closed in 1950. John White & Son Weighing Machines Ltd is still there, producing an extensive range of weighing machines for the 21st century, a manufacturer that has bridged the historical development of 'Muchty' for almost 300 years!

Ceres

Two miles south-east of Cupar, Ceres, possibly named after Saint Cyrus, is a village with a central village green, unusual in Scotland. It became a burgh of barony in 1620 under the control of the Hopes of Craighall. Gordon's map of 1642 (see endpaper at front of book) shows a bridge across the Craighall Burn, probably the narrow packhorse bridge that exists today. By 1750 Ceres was at the heart of a fully developed road system, with roads turnpiked by 1807. In 1790 locally grown flax was spun and woven by weavers. Around 800 people were making dowlas and sheeting in 1839, for Dysart manufacturers.

Above. Ceres Fair c.1900

Below. The village green is central to the community 2011

In the High Street of Ceres is the figure known as 'The Provost', a 19th-century carving by local stonemason John Howie (1820–1890). Re-erected in 1939, it is said to represent Thomas Buchanan, minister of Ceres 1578–99, and last holder of the office. Beneath the statue is a Howie panel thought to commemorate the Battle of Bannockburn in 1314. Two Annual Fairs were held in March and October. There was also a two-day event in June, the first day a market and the second a Fair or Games that still impacts on the community today. Ceres Games are the oldest free games in Scotland, held on the last Saturday of June, thought to have been held every year (except war years) since the charter to hold the games was granted to the village by Robert the Bruce in 1314. Today the village is home to the successful Fife Folk Museum, housed in the original 17th-century Weigh House.

Above. Ceres, looking south 2011

Left. 'The Provost', High Street, Ceres 2010

Vincenzo Lunardi

South of Pitscottie, east of Ceres, is the farm 'Coaltown of Callange', where a plaque records the landing of Lunardi and his balloon in 1785, after his first flight in Scotland. The Italian aeronaut had ascended from Edinburgh's Heriot's Hospital, George Heriot's School, and piloted his balloon the 46 miles across the Firth of Forth to touch down in Fife. The inscription records 'the first aerial voyage in Scotland'. The first balloonist to fly in Scotland was James Tytler, a minister's son from Fern in Angus. In 1784 he made a short half-mile voyage from Comely Garden to Restalrig, in Edinburgh. However, Lunardi is credited with making five voyages in Scotland, including the first aerial voyage from Scotland to England on 22 October 1785, when he ascended from Kelso and landed at Doddington Moor, Northumberland. Lunardi was a flamboyant character who had the distinction of being the first to view 'Fife from Above'!

Top. The farm Coaltown of Callange 2011

Above. Plaque at Coaltown of Callange farm 2011

Right. Lunardi's balloon

Above. Collessie Post Office c.1920

Below. Collessie 2011

Collessie

The small village of Collessie, almost 3 miles east of Auchtermuchty, still has some former 18th and 19th-century weavers' cottages, overlooked by a large square-towered parish church, built in 1838–39. The railway station in this former agricultural community opened in 1848 and closed in 1955. The railway track can be seen travelling from the base of the photograph to the top right. The Post Office closed in the early 1970s when the population was around 300. In recent times houses have been built, but the population today is now less than 200.

Cupar

Cupar is a community that over the centuries has benefited from its central location in the Howe of Fife, a route intersection from Falkland, St Andrews, Dundee and Kirkcaldy. On the winding River Eden this former County Town is thought to have grown around the site of Cupar Castle, the seat of the sheriff and owned by the earls of Fife. Chartered as a Royal Burgh in 1214 and re-chartered in 1327, it has records of wool exports in the early 14th century to Flanders and the Baltic. A Dominican priory was founded in 1348, two years prior to the Black Death that abruptly stopped the export of wool. However, by 1400 the wool trade had resumed, contributing to the peak of Cupar's international trade, during 1427–31, when it was eighth in Scotland. Despite trading links with Danzig in the 1440s, international trade declined. By 1564 the town had a grammar school and in the early 1600s an established farmers' market.

At this time the original part of the now listed Preston Lodge was built by the Laird of Airdrie; 1623 is inscribed on a stone on the west wall. Extended and remodelled over the years by James and William Preston, the original design is thought to have been inspired by Culross Palace.

By the 1650s there was commercial brewing, and a Post Office existed by 1715. Linen manufacturing and bleaching started in 1727, with the town having an incorporation of weavers around 1730. As agriculture developed in its hinterland, Cupar grew in importance as a market centre. By the late 1700s it was an important weaving centre with over 200 handlooms weaving over 500,000 yards of fabric, many bleached locally at a field near the River Eden. By the early 1800s the production had doubled.

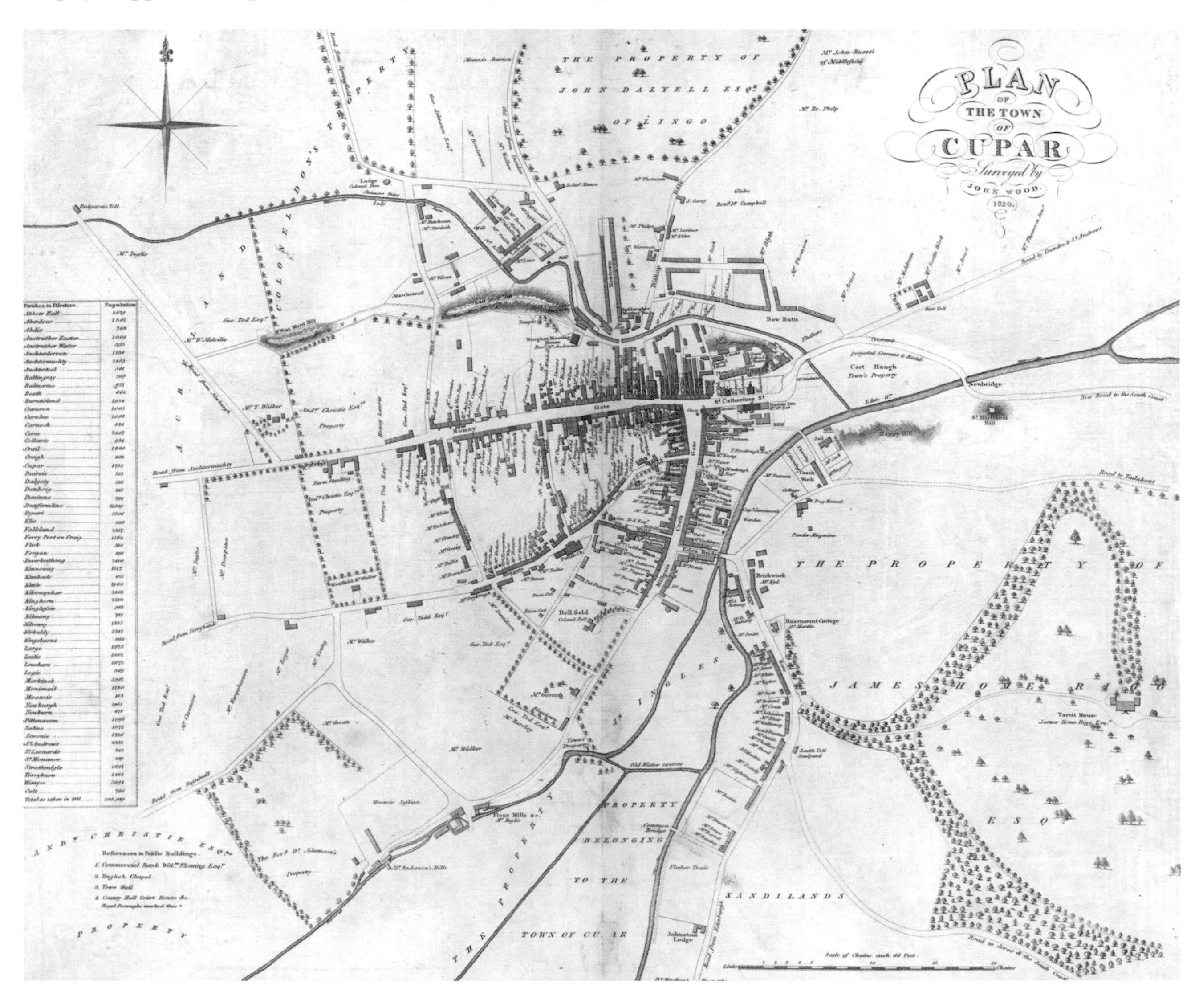

Map of Cupar by John Wood 1820

Cupar, looking west 1948

A Parish Church
B Stratheden Hospital
C St John's Church
D Corn Exchange
E Fife & Forfar Yeomanry Headquarters
F Braehead Housing Estate
G Fluthers
H County Buildings
I Haugh Park
J River Eden
K Railway Station
L Cupar Mill

Cupar 1966

Above.
A Gas Works
B Moat Hill
C Preston Lodge
D Bell Baxter
E Kinloss Park

Opposite.
A William Watt, Seed Merchants (former prison)
B Site of Castle
C Auction Mart
D Cross
E Bonnygate
F Fluthers
G Haugh Park

The imposing County Buildings, designed by Robert Hutchison, were erected between 1812 and 1817. A local press, which functioned between 1803 and 1849, was founded by Robert Tullis, who also established the Markinch paper mills. Cupar's local newspaper, the *Fife Herald* dates from 1822. By 1836 three flax-spinning mills had over 200 employees, while ten firms engaged some 600 weavers. 1847 saw the opening of the Edinburgh & Northern Railway (E&NR) between Cupar and Burntisland. By 1850 the line was completed to Tayport, Dundee and Broughty Ferry by the successors to E&NR, the Edinburgh, Perth and Dundee Railway. Cupar Golf Club was founded in 1855 with a nine-hole hillside course. The present Corn Exchange was built in 1861–62. The water-powered Russell Mill, owned by Smith, Laing & Co., in 1864 contained 2,200 spindles, looked after by over 200 workers, while the Cupar Mill, owned by William Smith, employed close on 100 workers. Around 1867, spinning ceased in Cupar but weaving continued. Flag and banner making is the specialism of the long-lasting Stratheden Linen Mills, established in 1866 by David Martin Stenhouse. The area known as the Fluthers was used for archery.

Bell Baxter High School, originally called Madras Academy, was founded in 1889–90 by St Andrews native the Rev. Dr Andrew Bell, when the Academy combined with the Sir David Baxter's Institute for Young Ladies. The school moved to new buildings in 1962 and acquired a new extension at Westfield Road in 1992.

Cupar 1982

As a consequence of the Beet Sugar Subsidy Act of 1925 a large beet sugar refining factory operated at Preston Hall from 1926 until 1972. From the early 1950s, with a population of around 6,000, the town provided a wide range of services. D.S. Honeyman & Co. produced linen until around 1958; the Elmwood Agricultural College opened in 1956.

Cupar was the former County Town of Fife until 1974, when the newly elected Fife Regional Council set up its headquarters in Glenrothes New Town. However, in 1975, Cupar did become the headquarters to North East Fife District, in preference to the larger and more historic St Andrews. This lasted until 1996 prior to a merger into a new single-tier Fife Authority.

Today the historic centre of the town is where the Bonnygate and Crossgate meet, marked by the original shaft of the late 17th century mercat cross. A community with a population of almost 9,000 provides a wide range of services within the prosperous Howe of Fife: rural living with the convenience of city facilities, linked by road and rail.

Previous pages. Cupar, looking down Kirk Wynd, centre of photograph, 2007

Looking west along St Catherine Street, Bonnygate and West Port 2007

Right. Sugar Beet factory at Preston Hall 1968

Below. Cupar commercial/retail park 2007

Falkland

Falkland was Scotland's first conservation area in 1970, a village in the shadow of the Lomond Hills, north of Fife's 'New Town', Glenrothes. The name is thought to be Old English, meaning 'Falconland', in boar and stag hunting country, where the Macduff Earls of Fife in the 12th or 13th century built themselves a hunting castle or tower. It is probable that the merciless Regent Albany had acquired this as a royal property by the early 1400s, to be reconstructed as a royal hunting palace. The surrounding village was probably a burgh of barony, before being chartered as a Royal Burgh in 1458. When French Master Mason Nicholas Roy undertook major reconstruction of the Palace for James V, a fine royal tennis court was built in 1539, now the oldest in the world. However, the palace suffered owing to a lack of maintenance after James V's death, but it was still used as a hunting base for James VI in the early 17th century. The Great Hall lost its roof in 1654, destroyed by Cromwellian troops. This damage was not repaired, despite the Palace remaining Crown property.

The village, like many other Fife communities, was a centre for hand-weaving of linens, chiefly coarse linens. By 1797 Falkland was a post town, with seven annual fairs, where the majority of the 1,000 population were employed in the productive agricultural hinterland.

Falkland Palace fell into ruin around 1790, but restoration started in 1823. Further restoration was undertaken from 1887 by the Crichton Stuarts, who became its hereditary keepers. Around 1860, John Scott constructed the small St Johns spinning mill and power-loom linen factory. It then became a floorcloth works around 1900. It was acquired by the Scottish Co-operative Wholesale Society in the early 1920s and then extended into a linoleum factory around 1930, to be finally closed in 1966. By 1988, Smith Anderson had ownership of the St Johns works, producing bags from paper and plastic. Today the Falkland site employs over 200 people as one of Europe's leading businesses in the packaging marketplace. In 1952 the National Trust for Scotland became the administrator of its only Royal Palace. A much-valued exhibit is the set of 17th-century Flemish 'verdure' tapestries that were acquired in 1906, by Lord Ninian Crichton Stuart, from an old house in Maarssern, Holland. Along with the recreation of the fine garden, this property has become a major tourist attraction for Fife. Ninian Crichton Stuart, grandson of the original buyer, is the current keeper. Falkland village still reflects much of its medieval charm and character.

Opposite. John Slezer's *The Prospect of Falkland from the East* 1693. The Lomond Hills are in the background. This view also has travellers on the road, a shepherd with livestock, and grazing horses.

Above. Falkland with Smith Anderson factory in foreground and Falkland Palace at top of photograph 2011

Left. Falkland Palace and grounds 2003

Firth of Tay

This image, from Tentsmuir, captures the narrow mouth of the Firth of Tay where sandbanks are an ever-present hazard for shipping.

Freuchie

The village of Freuchie lies 2 miles east of Falkland, at the foot of the Lomond Hills. By the mid 1800s William Lumsden & Son had built a power-loom factory, Eden Valley Works, which contained 100 looms and employed 320 handloom weavers. The Lumsden Memorial Hall was built in 1883. The mid 1800s also witnessed the building of Freuchie Corn Mill, combining a four-storey corn mill and a five-storey pyramid-roofed kiln, converted to residential use by the 1990s. The Lomond Hills Hotel dates from 1753.

Freuchie, looking east 2011. The A92 runs diagonally from top left of photograph

Hill of Tarvit

Formerly Wemyss Hall or Upper Tarvit, this house is situated on the south-facing slopes of Tarvit Hill, south of Cupar. Architect Sir Robert Lorimer incorporated parts of the 17th-century mansion house into his design of the house, for the jute magnate and collector F.B. Sharp. When the house was completed between 1905 and 1906, the main rooms were planned to suit the wonderful collection of Sharp's furniture. Now owned by the National Trust for Scotland, the house has been recently restored, to mark its centenary. The house is surrounded by 112 hectares of gardens, woods and parkland.

Hill of Tarvit 2011

Kettlebridge

Kettlebridge lies south of the River Eden on the A914 road between Glenrothes and Cupar. The community developed after the construction of the turnpike road c.1800 and the opening of the railway to Cupar in 1831. The bridge was built in 1831. Like neighbouring Kingskettle, Kettlebridge was a centre of the linen trade.

Kettlebridge in the foreground with Kingskettle to the rear 2011

Kilmany

This old fermtoun village is 4 miles north of Cupar on the A92 at the location of a memorial to Jim Clark, World Motor Racing Champion in 1963 and 1965. It was at Wester Kilmany Farm that the motor racing legend spent his first six years until 1942. Jim attended the local school before moving with his family to Edington Mains Farm, Chirnside, Berwickshire. He was tragically killed in a motor racing accident at Hockenheim, Germany, in April 1968. The memories of his undoubted immense talent live on. The memorial was unveiled in 1997 by his close friend, fellow Scot and former World Motor Racing Champion, Sir Jackie Stewart, OBE.

Above. Wester Kilmany Farm and the village of Kilmany 2011

Right. Jim Clark Memorial 2011

Kingskettle 2011

Kingskettle

In the Howe of Fife, south of the River Eden, ¾ mile south-east of Ladybank, lies Kingskettle. The town was originally called Catul or Katel, thought to refer to an ancient unrecorded battle, on ground that belonged to the Crown, hence King's Kettle or Kingskettle. It is a community that was home to handloom weavers and artisans in the late 18th and early 19th centuries.

Ladybank

Five miles south-west from Cupar, a small settlement was built on land that was previously drained and called Ladybog. The Edinburgh & Northern Railway created Ladybank Junction in 1846–47. A station and locomotive workshops were built, resulting in the development of a new settlement, laid out on a grid plan and named Ladybank. The village was designated a burgh in 1878, and by the early 1880s it had five insurance agencies, two hotels, a public hall, a branch of the Union Bank, malting and linen industries. The local golf club was founded in 1879, the original six-hole course being designed by Old Tom Morris. The waterworks were located in Beeches Road with a pumping tower, dated 1908.

Ladybank 1965

A Church of Scotland
B Hill Street
C Waterworks
D Railway Workshops
E Line to Cupar
F Line to Perth

Ladybank, with the railway station top right, 2011

Leuchars

Six miles from St Andrews, in Fife's north-east corner, lies Leuchars, a medieval village with the parish church, St Athernase, at its centre. The 12th-century stone church, founded by St Athernase from County Kildare, is impressive, as was its castle built a century later. Earlshall Castle was built in the 16th century. Between 1794 and 1864 handloom weaving was the main trade. 1848 saw the Edinburgh–Perth–Dundee Railway opened from Cupar to a temporary terminus near Leuchars Church, and then extended to Tayport two years later. Leuchars Junction station opened in 1852 with the link to St Andrews. In 1878 it was the starting point of the new mainline to the Tay Rail Bridge.

As a consequence of the army buying flat land to the east of the junction in 1908, to test man-lifting kites, the present Air Base was established. The area's lack of fog was

Top. Leuchars with the parish church in the centre 2011

Leuchars RAF Station 1972

Above. St Athernase Parish Church, Leuchars 2010

also a major factor for the development of the long-established airfield. Soon Leuchars was swamped by RAF service housing. An Air–Sea Search and Rescue unit was established in the mid 1950s, and closed in 1993. Today the Air Base is still the major employer and crucial to the local economy.

Nearby Guardbridge on the north side of the River Eden acquired a railway station in 1852 when the line was built to St Andrews. By 1872 the newspaper industry had taken off and a papermill had been established in the village, using wood pulp to produce newsprint. At the beginning of the 21st century specialised papers were still produced, until receivership forced closure in 2008.

Leuchars airfield 2011

Newburgh

In the north-west corner of the Kingdom, on the Perth to Cupar road, this community was originally a small fishing village, made into a *nova-burgus* (new burgh) by Alexander III for the monks of 12th-century Tironensian Lindores Abbey. The first abbot, Guido, brought from Kelso, is credited with starting the building of the monastery, before his death in 1219. Newburgh became a Royal Burgh in 1631, but was not admitted to the Convention of Royal Burghs, nor indeed represented in Parliament. Prior to 1780 the village's main industry was handloom weaving of linen. By the 1790s, Perth exporters used Newburgh quay because the Fair City had silted up. By the 1830s, over 500 looms were making linens for around 12 small firms, mostly homespun yarn. 1891 saw the start of linoleum manufacturing by the Tayside Linoleum Co., replacing weaving as the main industry until closure in 1980. Up to the beginning of World War I a ferry plied to and from Port Allen. Prior to the 1930s pleasure steamers called at the pier as they sailed between Perth and Dundee. Today Newburgh is still a village with many local amenities, and is a popular retirement community.

Newburgh, May 1948

Newburgh, looking east 1970

A Tayside Floorcloth factory closed 1978 destroyed by fire 1980
B Baptist Church
C Laing Museum
D Tayside Institute
E Georgian House (Town Hall)
F Congregational Church
G War Memorial
H Bowling Green

Newburgh 1980. Tayside Floorcloth factory in the foreground.

Newburgh 2011. Centre foreground, former site of factory, with evidence (right foreground) of ridge and furrow ploughing, a method of cultivation in the medieval period and later.

Newport-on-Tay

Ferries from Newport-on-Tay have sailed across Firth of Tay since the early 12th century, providing one of the shortest routes from Aberdeen and Dundee to Edinburgh. A pier was constructed at Newport by the Guildry of Dundee in 1713–15. By the 1790s, houses were being built. When the ferry terminal and new pier were built in the early 1820s to the designs of Scottish engineer Thomas Telford, ferry steamboats were able to operate to and from Dundee.

Newport 1974

A Young's Garage
B Town Council Yard
C Stables for hotel
D Newport Primary School, closed 1970
E Congregational Church
F St Fillian's (Free) Church
G Church of Scotland (previously St Thomas)
H Blyth Hall
I Tayfield Estate

The resulting impact was that Newport became popular as a bathing resort and it sparked off the building of large grey whinstone houses for affluent Dundonians. For a brief period Newport had a local rail service starting in 1879, but the collapse of the original Tay Railway Bridge in the same year brought this to a halt. However, on the completion of the replacement bridge in 1887 the village once again had a rail link to Dundee and became a police burgh. The two stations, East and West, closed in 1969, with the Tayport-to-Dundee branch line closing earlier, due to the construction of the approach roads to the Tay Road Bridge. The 20th-century vehicle ferry service became well established into the 1960s, a service that continued until the opening of the Tay Road Bridge in 1966. Today Newport is still a popular commuter town.

Newport with Tay Road Bridge 2011

Pitlessie

The village of Pitlessie lies 4 miles south-west of Cupar on the River Eden. This was where the painter Sir David Wilkie (1785–1841) first attended school; his home was the manse at nearby Cults. At the age of nineteen Wilkie demonstrated his remarkable ability by completing the subject-picture *Pitlessie Fair*, which includes around 140 figures, amongst whom are thought to be neighbours and several members of his family. The subject matter was a radical departure from the established conventions of history painting, reflecting the influence of 17th-century Dutch and Flemish paintings. Wilkie subsequently gained numerous prestigious commissions.

Above. Pitlessie Fair by David Wilkie 1804

Below. Pitlessie 2011

Scotstarvit Tower

Scotstarvit Tower is 2 miles south of Cupar. It was probably built in the late 15th or early 16th century for the Inglis family and then sold to Sir John Scot in 1611, a keen antiquarian who wrote *The Staggering State of the Scots Statesman* (published in 1754). As the Director of Chancery, a Lord of Session and a Privy Councillor, Sir John was clearly interested in Scotland's heritage and culture. The detailed map and survey of Fife in 1642 (see endpaper at front of book) was the result of a request from Scot of Scotstarvit to the cartographer James Gordon, Minister of Rothiemay, Banffshire.

Scotstarvit Tower 2011

Strathmiglo

The village of Strathmiglo, with a population of under 1,000, lies 15 miles south-east of Perth, on the upper reaches of the River Eden and north of the Lomond Hills. It is a community that became a burgh of barony in 1509. The landmark steeple dates from 1734. By the 19th century, with a population over 2,000, it was a thriving milling and weaving centre, supporting over 50 shops and businesses. 1857 saw the opening of the railway station. A.T. Hogg founded a small footwear factory in 1888. The Royal Cinema opened in 1929 and closed in the 1970s. The station closed in 1963. Today there is a primary school, food stores, a garage and light engineering.

Strathmiglo looking east 2011

Tay Road Bridge

The Tay Road Bridge is 1.4 miles long and spans the estuary between Dundee and Newport-on-Tay. The bridge was opened in 1966 at a cost of £4.8 million, designed by William A. Fairhurst, with main contractors Duncan Logan (Contractors) Ltd, Muir of Ord.

Right. Tay Road Bridge from Newport 2010

Below. The Tay Road Bridge links Dundee's city centre to Newport-on-Tay 2010

Tay Rail Bridge

The first railway bridge at this Wormit-to-Dundee crossing was completed in 1878. The Tay Bridge Disaster occurred in December 1879 when the central structure collapsed, taking with it a train and all 75 passengers and crew. All that remains are the stumps of piers, alongside the present structure and visible on the east side of the bridge. The current double-track crossing is approximately 2.25 miles long, designed by William H. Barlow, and opened in 1887.

Right. Tay Rail Bridge from Wormit 2010

Below. Tay Rail Bridge 2008

Tayport

On the northern shore of Fife at the mouth of the Firth of Tay, opposite Broughty Ferry, this community was originally known as Ferry-Port-on-Craig. This Tayside village was granted a burgh of barony charter in 1598. In the late 18th century the village's population increased dramatically owing to tenants settling here, having been displaced by agricultural improvements and clearances. By 1847 the Edinburgh & Northern Railway had built the Tayport harbour to accommodate the massive iron

Tayport 1969

A High Street
B Sawmill wood yard
C Tayport Primary School
D Donaldson Saw Mill
E Cinema
F Library
G Bowling Green

paddle steamers, fitted with rails for train wagons. This service operated to and from Broughty Ferry, part of the route from Edinburgh to Aberdeen. Rather than call the village Ferry-Port-on-Tay, the railway company called the community Tayport. The ferry ceased to operate on the opening of the first Tay Rail Bridge in 1878, resuming the following year after the collapse of the Rail Bridge. When the replacement bridge opened in 1887, Tayport reverted to a passenger-only ferry, until it ceased operation in 1920.

A limited amount of shipbuilding took place in the mid 1800s. A jute mill was founded in 1864 and survived into the 1920s. By 1867 around 200 people were employed in three flax, jute and hemp factories. The Tayport Engine Works, built by James Scott in 1875, manufactured marine and land engines, machinery for pumping, mining, ore separation and electrical plant. Most were exported, with the works closing in 1919 as the new owners moved to Dundee. Artist Martin Anderson, pseudonym 'Cynicus', returned to Tayport in 1898 and founded the Cynicus Publishing Co. Ltd in 1902, to produce his famous postcards, which reflected many topics. The company was an important employer but sadly the business collapsed in 1911.

Left. A selection of Cynicus postcards

Below and opposite. Tayport 2011

Tentsmuir

Tentsmuir Forest sits beyond the Eden Estuary, with Tayport in the background and the high flats of Dundee on the opposite side of the Firth of Tay. Note the group of grey seals, left foreground (also shown in the inset). This area encompasses the Tentsmuir National Nature Reserve and the Eden Estuary Local Nature Reserve. There are numerous waymarked walks and cycle routes through the pine trees of Tentsmuir.

Tentsmuir 2010

Wormit

Only a few houses existed at the southern end of the first Tay Rail Bridge, when it opened in 1878. The railway station, which generated the development of houses on the branch line to Newport, closed in 1969. The former Wormit station building is now the location of the ticket office at West Lothian's Bo'ness station, for the Scottish Railway Society's Bo'ness-to-Kinneil Railway. Wormit makes claim to be the first Scottish village to have installed electricity by using a windmill, situated on Wormit Hill, supplemented by a steam (later coal-gas) generator, until the 1930s, when it joined the National Grid. Wormit is a commuter base for Dundee, initially because of the rail link, and now because of the Road Bridge. Along with Newport-on-Tay and Woodhaven, Wormit is part of the Burgh of Newport-on-Tay.

Right. Tay Rail Bridge with Wormit Station in foreground c. 1902

Below. Wormit 2011

St Andrews

St Andrews

For close on 1,000 years St Andrews has been a destination for travellers. The great Cathedral, probably founded in 1162, with its shrine to St Andrew, was a place of pilgrimage. The 15th century witnessed the foundation of the University, a magnet now for thousands of students. The same era saw the first golf enthusiasts playing The Links, at what has now become the 'Home of Golf', a major tourist attraction.

In the mid 8th century a religious community contributed to the establishment of a settlement at what was then called Cennrigmonaid or Kilrymont. The burgh of St Andrews was founded out of this

settlement in the 12th century under the auspices of Bishop Robert, with permission from King David I.

There are a number of legends about the arrival of the relics of St Andrew. One legend is that an angel appeared to a Greek monk, named St Regulus (or St Rule) during the 4th or 5th century and told him to remove the bones of early Greek martyr St Andrew to 'the ends of the earth' for

Opposite. Townscape with St Andrews Bay, East Sands and West Sands 2010

Below. Map of St Andrews by John Wood 1820

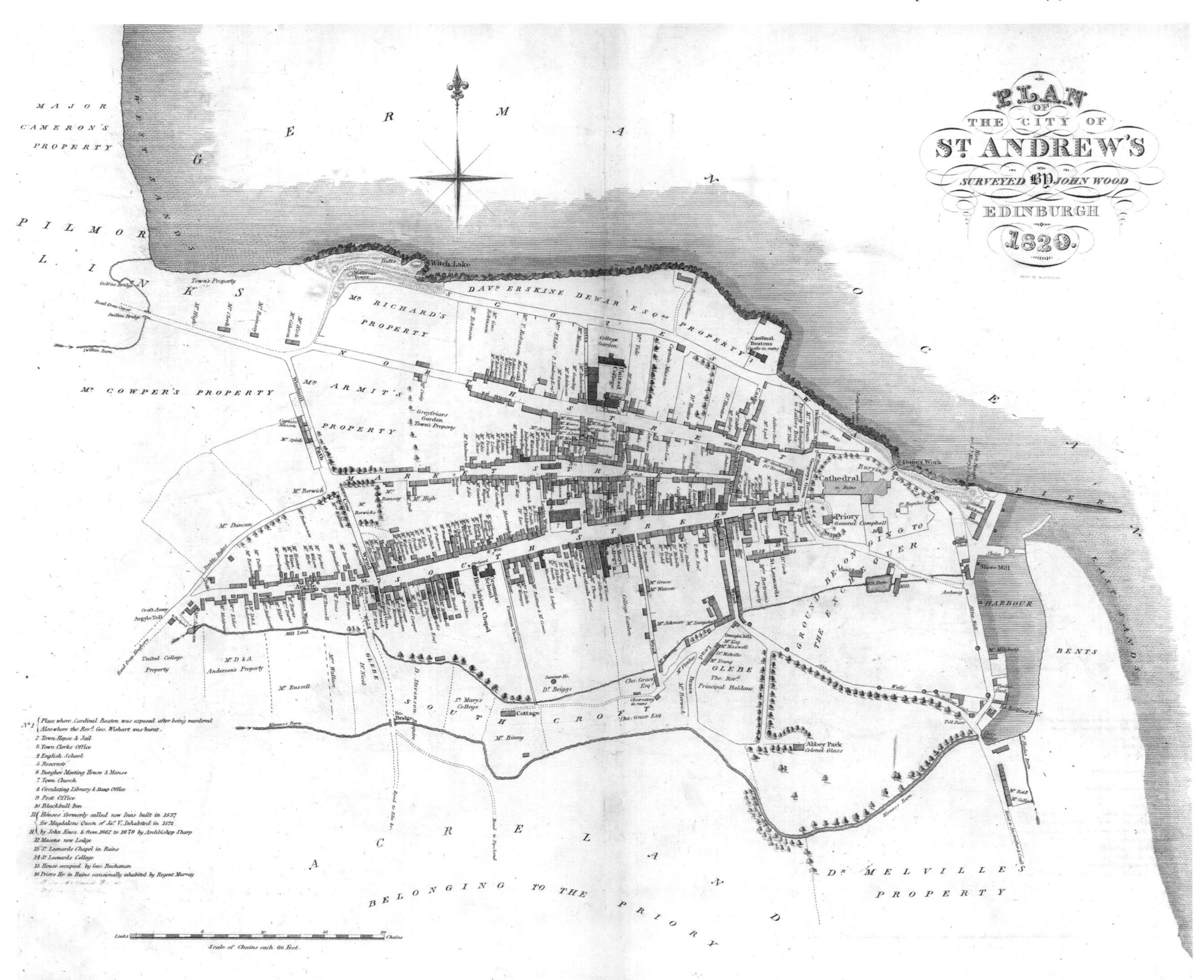

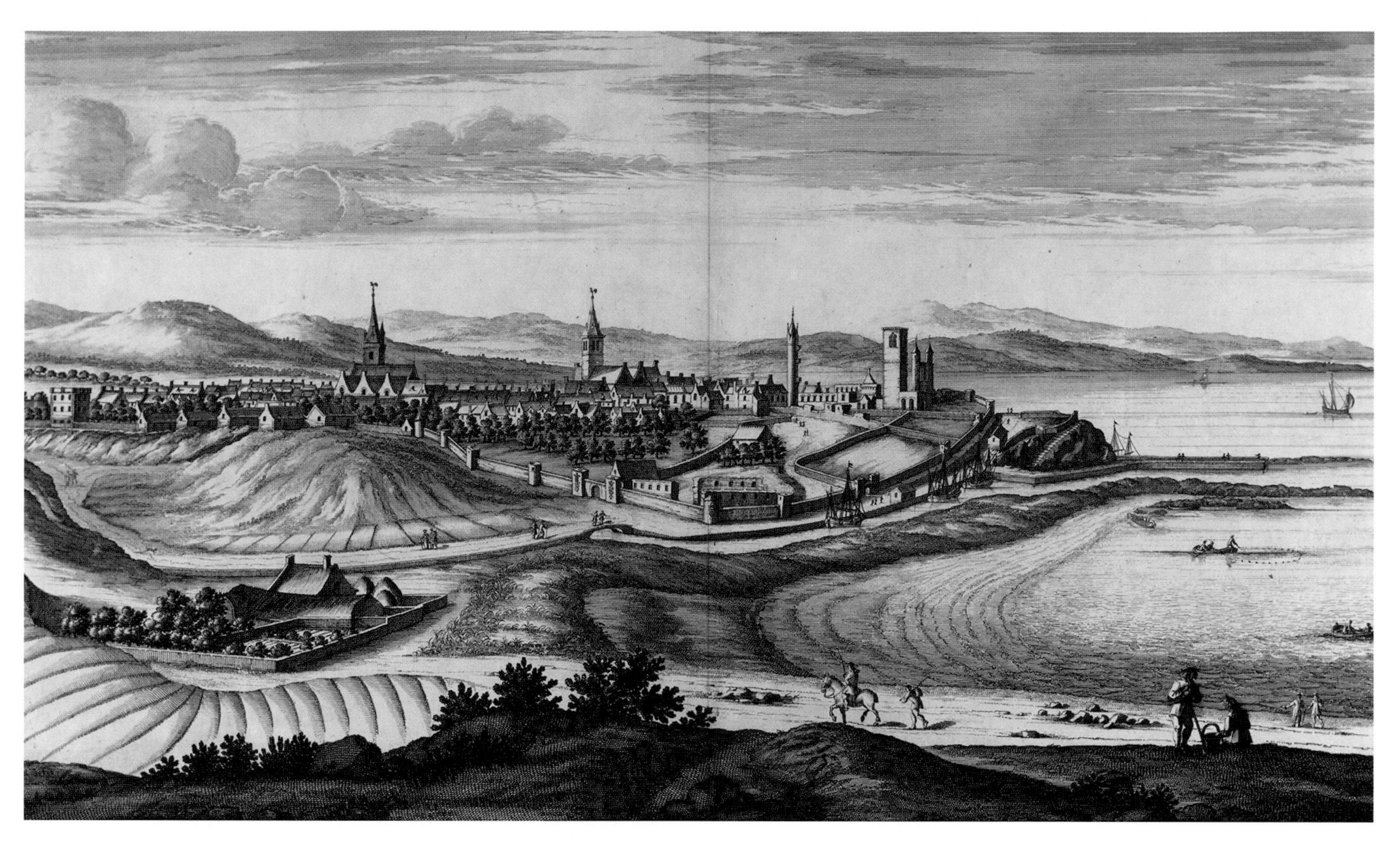

John Slezer's *The prospect of the Town of St Andrews* 1693. This general prospect was taken from the Kinkell Braes, showing the harbour, with ships and the cathedral within its encircling walls, which remain little changed today. The tower in the centre is the Chapel of St Salvator, while that to the left belongs to Holy Trinity, the parish church.

safety. St Rule removed some of the bones from St Andrew's tomb in Constantinople and brought them to Scotland. Shipwrecked, he came ashore on Fife's east coast, where he built a shrine to house the relics, presumably at modern Kirkhill. As to the truth of the legend, and whether Rule was a Greek monk, we shall never know.

By 908 Kilrymont had become the seat of the Bishop of Alba (Gaelic for Scotland) and Scotland had adopted Andrew as its Patron Saint, with an X-shaped motif, reflecting the wooden cross on which it is said he died. David I could be responsible for renaming this small community, with its tiny natural harbour, St Andrews. St Rule's Church, the tower of which survives today, was probably built c.1125–50 on the site of an older church by Bishop Robert when he founded the Augustinian Priory there. It was Arnold, Bishop of St Andrews who founded the new Cathedral in 1160, which was finally consecrated in 1318 by Bishop Lamberton in the presence of King Robert the Bruce. The ruin we see today is evidence of a magnificent Cathedral that was originally around 320 ft in length, increasing to about 390 ft. This magnificent church, Scotland's largest Cathedral and one of the most celebrated across Europe, was a centre of pilgrimage for thousands. This in turn involved St Andrews with events of the Protestant Reformation, resulting in the Cathedral being pillaged in 1559 by a mob organised by a group of Protestant lords. The buildings were left intact but this action ended 400 years of continuous worship, to be replaced by Holy Trinity Church as the main place of worship in the town. The magnificent building was then just a quarry for dressed stone, convenient for harbour and house building. Today the Cathedral is managed by Historic Scotland.

St Andrews Castle, situated on a headland overlooking the bay, was reputedly erected by Bishop Roger c.1200. It was the main residence of the bishops and archbishops of St Andrews and was known as the 'Bishop's Palace'. This was one of the most important strongholds in Scotland and is associated with many historical events. Records show that on a number of occasions it was rebuilt, most significantly at the end of the 14th century and after the siege of 1546–57. It has been a state prison and a fortified castle. Cardinal Beaton was murdered there (May 1546) because he was responsible for George Wishart, a protestant preacher, being burned at the stake in front of St Andrews Castle

Map of St Andrews by John Geddy c.1580. This 16th-century street plan is credited to John Geddy, a St Andrews academic and mathematician, who may well have tutored Timothy Pont. The Chapel of St Salvator, the Cathedral and the Castle with roof, all significant buildings of the town, were deliberately enlarged. The main east–west streets were straightened, perhaps to enhance this valuable depiction of the townscape.

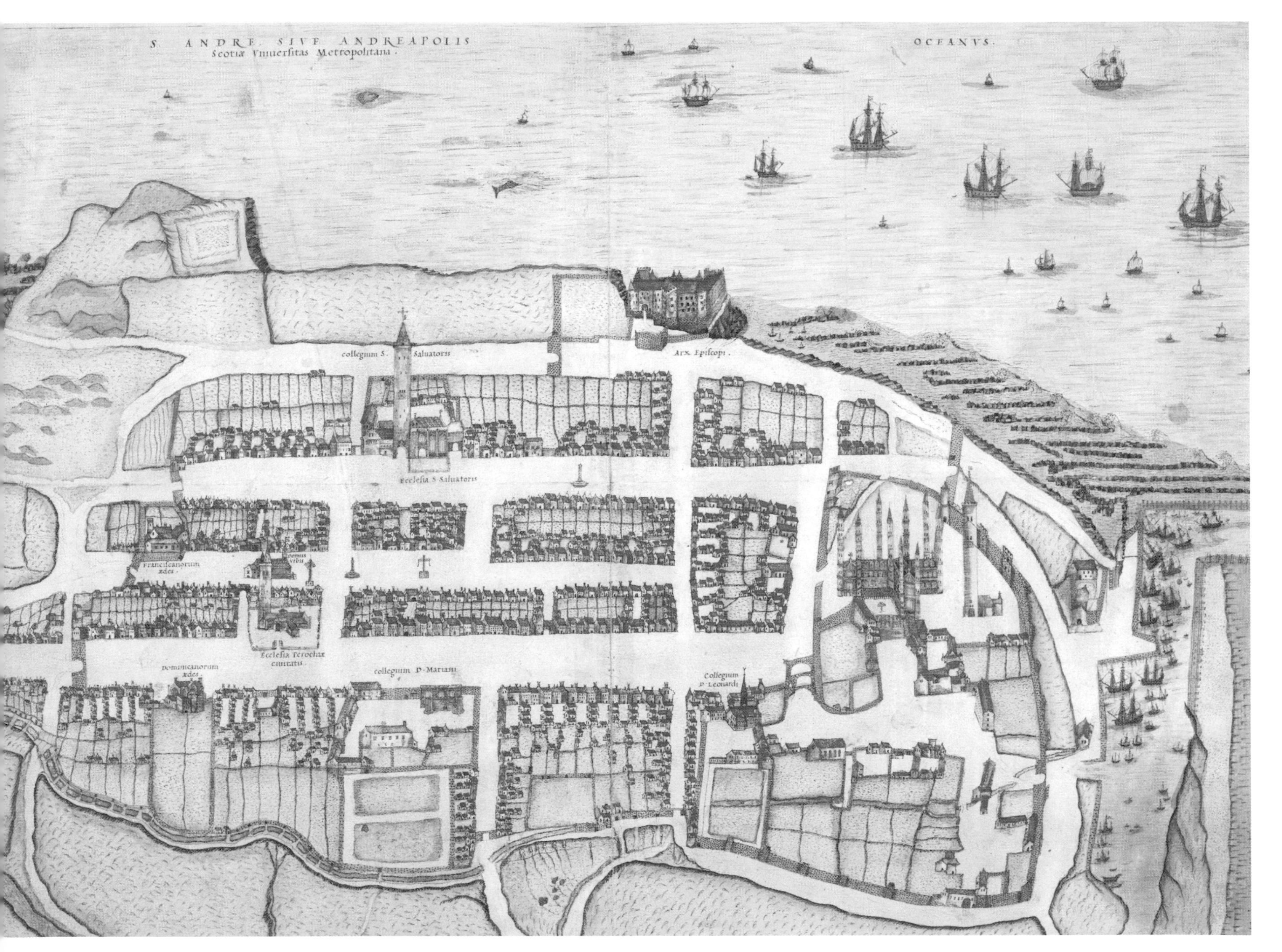

(March 1546). Historic Scotland manage this attraction. Note the roof of the Castle in Geddy's c.1580 map.

Martyr's Monument, to the rear of the Royal and Ancient Clubhouse, is one of the town's most prominent landmarks, built in 1842 to commemorate a number of Protestant figures who were martyred in the town between 1527 and 1558. This memorial records the important role St Andrews played in the Reformation. Those who were killed for their Protestant beliefs include the following. Patrick Hamilton was an outspoken Scottish nobleman who was burned at the stake outside St Salvator's Chapel in 1528. Hamilton's initials can be found in the cobblestones on North Street, marking the spot where he died. Henry Forrest was executed in 1533 for speaking out against the killing of Patrick Hamilton. Forrest was burned at the highest point in St Andrews, outside the north end of the Cathedral. George Wishart was martyred outside St Andrews Castle in 1546. Wishart's initials are set in stone into the road overlooking Castle Sands, the spot where he was burned. Less than three months later, Beaton was murdered by a group of Protestant Reformers posing as workmen. Walter Milne (or Myln) was 83 years old when he was executed outside the north side of the Cathedral. Some accounts suggest that he may have been burned at the stake because he believed that Catholic priests should be permitted to marry.

Around 1150 St Andrews was granted burgh status from Bishop Robert with the permission of David I. By 1614 it was a Burgh of Regality and in 1620 James VI confirmed it as a Royal Burgh.

By the end of 1500s, the medieval period, Trade Guilds dominated the commercial life of the community. Bakers, fleshers, shoemakers, smiths, tailors, weavers and wrights, all reflected quality standards.

The town's medieval buildings and the striking domestic architecture of the 16th, 17th and 18th centuries are second only to the Old Town of Edinburgh within Scotland. No evidence exists of St Andrews being a walled city. However, during the troubles of the 1500s the outer streets and wynds were closed by gates or ports. The only remaining port is the West Port with its arch, at the end of South Street, although this was changed in 1843. The transformation of the medieval city to a modern town was influenced by Provost Sir Hugh Lyon Playfair (1786–1861). Noted local architect George Rae, born 1811, designed North Bell Street (1834–36), South Bell Street (1848–58) and Playfair Terrace, which nearly bankrupted the town council, making them try to sell off the Links. Rae is also credited with designing in the 1850s the Union Club, later the R & A Clubhouse, and some of Queen's Gardens in the 1860s.

The railway arrived in 1852 from Leuchars Junction and had a major impact, making the town a popular seaside resort. Hotels were built for accommodation, including the Rusack's Marine Hotel, completed in 1891. In the 1930s the open-air swimming pool

Martyr's Monument c. 1917

St Andrews, viewed from the Links, June 1949

A Railway Station
B Old Course 18th fairway
C Royal and Ancient Clubhouse
D Martyr's Monument
E Open-Air Swimming Pool
F The Scores
G Chapel of St Salvator

St Andrews from the south-east, June 1949

A St Salvator's
B St Leonards School
C Grange Road
D Burgh School
E Football pitch
F Medical Buildings
G Railway

was constructed. The railway closed in 1969, but with improved road links, an exceptional location and the increased popularity of golf, the town continues to thrive as a holiday destination and as an attractive, convenient town in which to live. The 1980s and 1990s witnessed an increase in private housing developments.

The harbour, on the estuary of the Kinness Burn, dates from the 13th century. By the late 19th century, fishing engaged around 200 men; crabs and herring were caught with just under 60 boats, based at the small harbour. However, as boats became larger and more expensive, fishing activities declined. There are still a few boats creel fishing for crab and lobster. Still retaining its medieval form, the main pier frequently captures the traditional after-Sunday-service walk of the red-gowned 21st-century students.

The first Botanic Garden in the town was laid out by Dr John Wilson from 1889, in a quarter of an acre of walled garden, south of St Mary's College in South Street. 1960 saw the relocation to the present site at Bassaguard. In 1987 the University leased the Garden to North East Fife District Council, now Fife Council, with responsibility for its management.

The University of St Andrews, the first university in Scotland and third oldest in the English speaking world, after Oxford and Cambridge, was founded by the Bishop of St Andrews, Henry Wardlaw, with full university status being conferred in 1413. By the 1550s the University had three colleges: St Salvator's (1450), St Leonard's (1512), and St Mary's (1539). The

Open-air swimming pool, St Andrews 1955

Botanic Gardens, St Andrews 2010

buildings of St Salvator's Chapel and St Mary's College date from the early 1500s. Between the 16th and 18th century St Salvator's and St Leonard's amalgamated to form the United College, which still survives in an enlarged form. Divinity, the Arts, the Physical and Biological Sciences all made considerable progress in the 19th century. By 1897 a new academic centre, University College Dundee, was founded and affiliated to St Andrews, providing links to Medical and Applied Science. University College Dundee was re-named the University of Dundee in 1967. Today the University of St Andrews is a major employer with approximately 1,800 staff, 700 academic and 1,100 support personnel, a crucial element of the local economy outwith the tourist season. It has 7,500 students, 6,000 being undergraduates.

The importance of the University of St Andrews as a catalyst for the development of photography in Scotland is attributed to Sir David Brewster, Principal of the United College in the early 1840s. He was instrumental in supporting the first experimental works in photography by John Adamson, resulting in the first successful photograph in Scotland, taken by John Adamson, in St Andrews, in 1842. Adamson imparted his photography skills to his much younger brother Robert, who went on to become one half of the famous photographic duo Hill & Adamson. In more recent years the University has become guardian to the photographic

James Wilson (1742–98)

Born in St Andrews, son of a local farmer, James studied at the University of St Andrews before emigrating to the American colonies in 1765. He gained a reputation as one of the country's leading political theorists. He is one of only six men to have signed both the American Declaration of Independence and the Constitution of the United States.

Above left. St Andrews from St Salvator's Chapel Tower c. 1918

Left. South Street, looking east c. 1905

Above. North Street and Chapel of St Salvator c. 1906

St Andrews, looking west 2007. University buildings including the Library and the Chapel of St Salvator. North Street dominates, with The Scores to the right.

archive of Valentines of Dundee, the well-known company which produced albums of Scottish views from the 1870s, and later became the producer of postcards. The University also holds the complete archive of Robert Moyes Adam, the Scottish landscape photographer, and the work of George Cowie, a local press photographer from 1930 to 1982. Today the Special Collections of the University houses one of the great photographic collections in the world, with over 700,000 photographs.

St Leonards School was called the St Andrews School for Girls in 1877, renamed St Leonards in 1883 and built on the former Cathedral grounds. St Katharines School for Girls provided education for under 14s and opened in 1894 in North Street, with boarding houses on The Scores; it moved to the grounds of St Leonards in 1970. This independent school is now co-educational with pupils from ages 5 to

18, known today as St Leonards School. The only state secondary school in the town is Madras College, which opened in 1832. It was based on a peer-support system that was developed by the school's founder and native of the town, the Rev. Dr Andrew Bell (1755–1832), when he was a chaplain to the East India Company in Madras. Madras College became comprehensive in 1963, with the Kilrymont Road annex, for younger pupils, opened in 1967.

St Andrews 2007. The harbour, the Cathedral precinct and the Castle are in the foreground as the town spreads west.

Tom Morris (1821–1908)

Born in St Andrews, Tom Morris (known as Old Tom Morris) is viewed as a pioneer of modern golf. His son, known as Young Tom Morris, won the Open on three occasions. He died aged 24 in 1875. After an apprenticeship at Prestwick, Old Tom was appointed Keeper of the Green at the Old Course in 1865 and was the first Honorary Professional to the R&A. He was a skilled club and ball maker with premises overlooking the 18th green of the Old Course. In addition he was a renowned greenkeeper and course designer; he established the practice of top-dressing greens, managing hazards and standardising course length to 18 holes, a reducation from St Andrews' original 23 holes. He won four Open Championships at Prestwick, in 1861, 1862, 1864 and 1867. The 18th hole of the Old Course is named in his honour. Tom Morris died aged 87 and is buried in St Andrews Cathedral grounds.

Top left. Old Tom Morris

Above left. Old Course, St Andrews 1905

Above. Morris gravestones

The Royal and Ancient Golf Club of St Andrews (R&A), renowned around the world, is a private club and the governing body of golf outside the USA. It has responsibilities for a number of major championships and reviews the Rules of Golf. It was the creation of the Society of St Andrews Golfers in 1754 that also records the origins of the club. On receiving the patronage of King William IV in 1834, the Society gained the title The Royal and Ancient Golf Club. The imposing clubhouse, much extended and modernised, has overlooked the Old Course since 1854. The Old Course, run by St Andrews Links Trust, has hosted the game for over six centuries. Not designed by any architect, it evolved out of the natural terrain of the Links. The British Golf Museum, located behind the R&A, traces the history of golf, both in Britain and across the world, from the Middle Ages to the present day. The St Andrews Links Courses are: Old (14th century), New (1895), Jubilee (1897), Eden (1914), Strathtyrum (1993), Balgove (1972) and Castle (2008).

St Andrews remains one of Scotland's most charming coastal towns, a community that reflects history of one thousand years, while still providing a unique environment for recreation and study.

Top. The Royal and Ancient Clubhouse 2011

Left. 18th fairway bridge, Old Course, St Andrews 2010

Old Course hotel, foreground, along with the first and final holes of the Old Course, a familiar scene to golfers world-wide. 2010

St Andrews 2010. World renowned golf links, with the estuary of the River Eden and Leuchars airfield in the distance.

Islands of Fife

Island of Inchcolm

This prominent Firth of Forth feature, within Fife, lies 1½ miles south-west of Aberdour. Inchcolm means 'Columba's Isle' although there is no known link to St Columba. In 1123 King Alexander I was shipwrecked on the island. He vowed to found a community of Augustinian monks but the plans were interrupted the following year by his death. It is not clear when the monastery was finally established, but an early charter dates from around 1162–69, and Augustinian Canons settled here, clearly attracted by the island's isolation and tranquility. Dominating the island is the Abbey complex, raised to full Abbey status in 1235. It became one of the most powerful and wealthy monastic communities in Scotland in the Middle Ages. After the Protestant Reformation of 1560, monastic life came to an end.

The 16th century saw the island being used as a state prison and a fort. During the Napoleonic Wars and the two World Wars it was fortified. The fine state of preservation of the buildings is mainly due to the isolated position of the island, now in the care of Historic Scotland.

Inchcolm Abbey 2011

Island of Inchcolm 2011

Island of Inchkeith 2011

Island of Inchkeith

Inchkeith is an island in the Firth of Forth, included within Fife, some 3 miles south-east of Kinghorn. It was once known as 'L'île des Chevaux' (Island of Horses), attributed to the French troops garrisoned there in the mid 16th century. Malcolm II, in 1010, granted the island to Robert de Keith (hence its present name), for his support in the battle against the Danes. During the 15th century it was a refuge for plague victims. In the 20th century it was used as a military base until after the end of World War II. The first lighthouse was built in 1803, with an automated light being established in 1986, thus making the island uninhabited and the historical monuments inaccessible and neglected. Today the island is privately owned.

Isle of May

At the entrance to the Firth of Forth, 5 miles south-east of Anstruther, lies the Isle of May. This 150 acre island had a monastic settlement in the 9th century when St Adrian established a retreat. In the 12th century King David I founded a monastery, and Benedictine monks were based here. By the early 14th century, interest in the island had waned and the focus was on the Priory of Pittenweem, which had been established as a refuge from Norse raiders centuries earlier. By 1549 the possessions of May had passed to the Augustinian Priory of St Andrews and the ecclesiastical buildings were lying in waste. Only a small 13th-century chapel remains. A beacon lighthouse began guiding mariners in 1636. A replacement, built by Robert Stevenson, was completed in 1816. Lights continued to be supervised and upgraded until 1989 when the light became automated. A National Nature Reserve since 1956, the Isle of May is home to a large breeding population of seabirds, including guillemots, shags, razorbills, kittiwakes and puffins. Scottish Natural Heritage own and manage the island.

Above. Isle of May 2011

Mugdrum Island

In the River Tay, close to Newburgh, is Mugdrum Island, covering around 40 acres. This is a low-lying area with North Deep to the north and South Deep to the south. It's now part of Balmyre Farm, Errol, and is used for grazing.

Mugdrum Island 2011

Bibliography

A.W. Brotchie *Fife's Trams & Buses* N.B. Tracton 1990
R.L. Brown *Fife in History and Legend* John Donald 2002
R.L. Brown *Discovering Fife* John Donald 1988
K. Cavers *Vision of Scotland* HMSO 1993
A. Darwood and P. Martin *The Milestones of Fife* East Fife Preservation Societies 2005
K. Ferguson *A New Town's Heritage* Glenrothes Development Corporation 1996
J. Gifford *Fife* Penguin 1992
J. Keay and J. Keay *Collins Encyclopaedia of Scotland* Harper/Collins 1994
B. McEwan *Dunfermline The Post War Years* Breedon Books 2009
M. K. Oglethorpe *Scottish Collieries* RCAHMS 2006
D. Omand *The Fife Book* Birlinn 2000
G.L. Pride *The Kingdom of Fife* Rutland Press 1999
R. Smith *The Making of Scotland* Canongate 2001
B. Walker and G. Ritchie *Fife, Perthshire and Angus* HMSO 1996

Picture Credits

© Aerial Photography Solutions: 2, 3, 4t, 7, 8, 10, 12–13, 15, 16, 17, 20, 26, 27, 31, 34, 35, 36t, 37, 40, 41, 42, 43t, 44, 45, 46, 49, 50b, 51, 52, 53, 57b, 58–9, 60b, 62b, 64, 65t, 71, 73, 74t, 75, 76b, 79b, 81, 83, 84, 85, 86, 87b, 89, 90, 91, 92, 93, 94–5, 96, 97, 100, 101, 102, 103t, 104b, 105t, 106t, 107b, 112–13, 114, 115b, 117, 118, 119, 120, 121, 122t, 123, 125, 126tl, 127, 130, 132, 133b, 134, 135b, 136b, 138, 139b, 140, 141b, 142, 155, 156–7, 158, 159, 160, 161, 162.

Author's collection: 1, 14br, 23c, 28tr, 29tl, 38b, 39b, 48br, 50tr, 62tr, 68br, 78tr, 87tr, 94bl, 103bl, c, 105br, 106c, 122br, 126bl, 135tr, 136tr, 139tl, tc, tr, 141tr, 146, 149b, 150, 153, 154.

Ian Campbell collection: 107tl.

© Courtesy of the Alan B. Carlaw Collection. Licensor www.scran.ac.uk: 126br.

Courtesy of the Andrew Carnegie Birthplace Museum, Dunfermline: 23br.

Crown Copyright, RCAHMS: 47t.

© Fife Council: 63, 78b, 82, 88, 98, 99.

© Fife Council Libraries and Museums Service, Dunfermline Carnegie Library, Local Library Collection: 9, 24, 25, 29, 30, 33, 36b, 39, 43b.

© Fife Council Libraries and Museums Service, Kirkcaldy Central Library, Local Library Collection: 69, 70, 72, 104tr, 110, 111, 124, 129, 131, 137.

Hulton Archive/Getty Images: 106br.

© J. Lewis: ii.

© Ian Mills, Photography, Crail (printed with permission of the Abbey Church of Dunfermline): 19tr.

© National Galleries of Scotland. Licensor www.scran.ac.uk: 133t.

Reproduced by permission of the Trustees of the National Library of Scotland: Fife maps front and back endpapers, 5, 11, 18, 19b, 66, 108, 116, 143, 144, 145.

© National Trust for Scotland / Douglas McGregor: 91br.

© National Museums Scotland. Licensor www.scran.ac.uk: 48bl, 68t, 74b.

© Newsquest (Herald & Times) Licensor www.scran.ac.uk: 149t.

© RCAHMS Licensor www.scran.ac.uk: 57t, 94tl.

© RCAHMS (Aerofilms Collection): 115t.

© RCAHMS (John Dewar Collection): 14t.

RCAHMS: National Collection of Aerial Photography/aerial.rcahms.gov.uk: 6, 21, 22, 32, 38, 54, 55, 56, 67, 76t, 77, 79t, 80, 109, 128, 147, 148.

© The Scotsman Publications Ltd. Licensor www.scran.ac.uk: 47bl, 61.

© Scottish Mining Museum. Licensor www.scran.ac.uk: 60t.

Courtesy of Scottish Viewpoint: 28b.

Courtesy of the University of St Andrews Library: Aerial 2: 151.

Courtesy of the University of St Andrews Library: Aerial 3: 152.

Johnstone Wood collection: 4bl, bc, br, 65bl.

Abbreviations:
t top, b bottom, c centre; tl top left, tc top centre, tr top right; bl bottom left, bc bottom centre, br bottom right.

Tobar an Dualchais/Kist o Riches Audio Links

To give an additional dimension to this publication I have identified a number of audio recordings associated with Fife on the online Tobar an Dualchais/Kist o Riches project. A headphone logo beside a community name indicates that there is an associated audio link. You can read more about the background to this project in the promotional section on page 167. The project is online at www.tobarandualchais.co.uk/

To proceed to a specific recording, enter: http://www.tobarandualchais.co.uk/fullrecord/ into your internet browser (along with the ID number provided and the suffix /1). For example to hear the song 'Isle of May' with ID number 85171 you would enter: http://www.tobarandualchais.co.uk/fullrecord/85171/1

The recordings that I have identified include contributions from Gary Coupland MBE, Dr Sheila Douglas, Cilla Fisher MBE, Isabella Redpath, James Redpath, Dr Jean Redpath MBE, Lucy Stewart, Artie Trezise MBE and John Watt. The reporters are Arthur Argo, Dr Margaret Bennett, Hamish Henderson, Ian Paterson and Stephanie Smith Perrin.

To listen to some of the material associated with Fife, reference should be made to the list on the right.

REFERENCE NUMBER	DESCRIPTION	FORMAT	TOWN
53344/1	Railway Station Porter	song	Auchtermuchty
78763/1	Tangle o' the Isles	dulcimer	Leven
78773/1	Bonny Bunch of Roses	song	Leven
78776/1	Queen Mary Queen Mary	song	Leven
78777/1	In and Out the Windows	song	Leven
78779/1	One, Two, Three a-leary	song	Leven
78782/1	Ball of Kirriemuir	song	Leven
78785/1	Down in the Meadow where the Green Grass Grows	song	Leven
78788/1	I sent a Letter to my Love	rhyme	Leven
78789/1	Oh Dear, Mother, What a Cold I've Got	rhyme	Leven
78799/1	Two Fife sayings		Leven
78800/1	A saying and anecdote about meanness		Leven
78801/1	Route of a bicycle ride in Fife	dialect	Leven
78802/1	Fife farm names and place names		Leven
78808/1	Fife sayings with explanations		Leven
78815/1	Maggie Murphy She Fell Drunk	song	Leven
78817/1	Clean Pease Strae	song	Leven
78818/1	Who'll Walk My Girl at Night?	song	Leven
78821/1	Some Fife sayings		Leven
78828/1	The New Highland Laddie	dulcimer	Leven
78840/1	James Redpath recalls playing dulcimer with cousin Willie Welch		Leven
78846/1	James Redpath talks about his grandfather's dulcimer		Leven
78847/1	James Redpath plays a waltz on dulcimer		Leven
76791/1	Jean Redpath demonstrates the fisher accent		Leven
76798/1	Fife accent and dialect		Leven
86375/1	Believe Me If All Those Endearing Young Charms	dulcimer	Leven
86377/1	Jig performed on dulcimer		Leven
86378/1	Uist Tramping Song	dulcimer	Leven
86379/1	Bells of Leven Episcopal Church	dulcimer	Leven
86389/1	Imph-m	song	Leven
86391/1	The Strange Wild Cry of Homeless Things	melody	Leven
67583/1	Michael Colliery	song	East Wemyss
94524/1	Pittenweem Jo	song	Pittenweem
94526/1	John Thomson	song	Cardenden
94527/1	The Kelty Clippie	song	Kelty
85171/1	The Isle of May	song	Isle of May

National Library Maps and Drawings

The following notes provide background on James Gordon, John Slezer and John Wood.

James Gordon, Minister and Cartographer

The 1642 map of Fife at the beginning of this book was compiled by James Gordon. James Gordon's father, Robert Gordon of Straloch, worked on updating Timothy Pont's maps for Johan Blaeu, the Dutch cartographer. On the death of Robert Gordon in 1661, all of Pont's surviving maps were preserved by his son James. Before his death in 1686 he presented his entire manuscript map collection to Geographer Royal, Sir Robert Sibbald, for a planned new Scottish atlas. The plan was to publish Pont's work, James and Robert Gordon's own activities, including the 1642 map (front endpaper), along with textual and topographical descriptions of Scotland. The atlas never materialised. However, the archive survived and was purchased by the Advocates Library in Edinburgh. By 1925, it was in the possession of the National Library of Scotland. Here the collection remains, a unique legacy preserved through the initial foresight and astute guardianship of Robert and James Gordon, 17th-century father and son cartographers.

John Slezer, Chief Engineer for Scotland

Most of the drawings and engravings completed in Fife by Slezer are included in this book. John Abraham Slezer is thought to have been born before 1650 in part of German-speaking Europe, and moved to Scotland in 1671 to take up a senior military post. Eventually securing the position of Chief Engineer for Scotland, his duties as Surveyor of His Majesties Stores and Magazines required him to report on the state of fortifications in Scotland. This task saw him making a collection of drawings and engravings of the most remarkable public and private buildings in Scotland, including Culross, Dunfermline, Falkland and St Andrews. During his travels he decided to produce a book of Scotland's main towns, castles and buildings.This was the first time anyone had made a pictorial record of an entire nation. The book was to be titled *Theatrum Scotiae*. With financial assistance from Scottish earls, Slezer arranged for the printing in London. He did proceed with other drawings but, as increased expenses and money promised from Parliament were not forthcoming, combined with the irregularity of army pay, he fell into considerable debt. Sadly, the last years of his life were spent in the debtor's sanctuary within the bounds of Holyrood Abbey in Edinburgh. Despite being a debtor he continued as Captain of the Train of Artillery of Scotland. He held the post until military re-organisation in 1716. John Slezer, 'recorder of the State of Scotland', died in 1717.

John Wood, surveyor and map-maker

John Wood, born c.1780/85, was the most significant surveyor of Scottish towns. He published 50 plans of Scottish towns between 1818 and 1826. A few of these plans, such as those for Edinburgh, Glasgow and Dundee, were based on recent town plans by other surveyors, but most were based on original surveys by Wood himself. As well as being published individually, 48 of these plans were also published in Wood's *Town Atlas of Scotland* (1828). Within Fife his work included Cupar and St Andrews, maps based on other surveyors' work. In the case of Burntisland, Dunfermline and Kirkcaldy, the resulting maps were based on his survey of the communities. Wood was resident in Edinburgh from 1813, and in the late 1820s and 1830s he surveyed English and Welsh towns. He returned to Edinburgh in the 1840s before his death in 1847.

Photograph, map and audio collections used in this book

Tobar an Dualchais/Kist o Riches

Tobar an Dualchais/Kist o Riches is a collaborative project set up to preserve, digitise and catalogue oral recordings from Shetland to the Borders and Fife to the Western Isles. Over 20,000 recordings are now available online at: http://www.tobarandualchais.co.uk/

The website has a wealth of material such as folklore, songs, music, history, poetry, traditions and stories, with the earliest recordings made in the late 1930s.

The recordings come from three major collections: the School of Scottish Studies (University of Edinburgh); BBC Scotland; and the National Trust for Scotland's Canna Collection.

The project will ensure that Scotland's rich oral history is safeguarded and made widely available for present and future generations.

References to recordings on the Tobar an Dualchais/Kist o Riches website are included in this book and use of these recordings is bound by the terms and conditions outlined on the website.

All the website references to Tobar an Dualchais/Kist o Riches material were live at the time of going to print but please note that, on the odd occasion, recordings may be removed from the website.

Tobar an Dualchais/Kist o Riches
Sabhal Mòr Ostaig
Sleat
Isle of Skye IV44 8RQ

Telephone: +44 (0) 1471 888603
Email: dualchas@smo.uhi.ac.uk

The National Library of Scotland

The National Library of Scotland is a reference library with world-class collections. NLS is also Scotland's largest library and one of the major research libraries in Europe. Our collections range from rare historical documents to online journals, covering every subject. We specialise in Scotland's knowledge, history and culture. We hold around 14 million printed items, over 100,000 manuscripts, around 2 million maps and 25,000 newspaper and magazine titles.

Anyone can get a library card to use National Library of Scotland collections and services. We support the work of academic researchers, although you do not need academic credentials to use NLS. We welcome a wide range of users. You can register online before your visit, which will shorten the time it will take to issue you with a library card when you visit. By registering online, you gain free access to an extensive range of licensed digital collections, including: reference works, newspapers, journals, digitised books and manuscripts. We are happy to assist with your research, please e-mail: enquiries@nls.uk

The National Library of Scotland has digitised thousands of items in our collection, including complete books, manuscripts, maps, photographs, posters and drawings. You can view these items through the digital gallery on our website.

http://www.nls.uk/digital-gallery

In particular, over ten thousand historical maps of Scotland have been digitised, including maps of Scotland, county maps, town plans and charts of the coastline. These can be viewed at: http://maps.nls.uk/. You are welcome to use these historical maps for personal research. If you have any queries, please contact maps@nls.uk and we will be happy to help.

National Library of Scotland
George IV Bridge
Edinburgh EH1 1EW
Telephone: 0131 623 3700
Website: www.nls.uk

The Royal Commission on the Ancient and Historical Monuments of Scotland

The publisher acknowledges the assistance of the Royal Commission on the Ancient and Historical Monuments of Scotland (RCAHMS) in the production of this volume. Many of the images in this volume have been selected from the RCAHMS collections. RCAHMS is responsible for collecting, recording and interpreting information on the architectural, industrial, archaeological and maritime heritage of Scotland. Whether you are working, teaching, studying or simply exploring your local heritage, RCAHMS resources are available to assist your research. Included in those resources is the national collection of aerial photography of Scotland that comprises over one million images, ranging in date from 1920 to 2000. The images have come from sources including the Royal Air Force, Ordnance Survey, private companies and the Luftwaffe, as well as from RCAHMS's own flying programme.

RCAHMS
John Sinclair House
16 Bernard Terrace
Edinburgh, EH8 9NX

Telephone: +44 (0) 131 662 1456
Email: info@rcahms.gov.uk
Website: www.rcahms.gov.uk

Public search room open:
Monday, group visits
Tuesday–Friday, 9.30am–5pm

scran

Scottish Cultural Resource Archive Network (SCRAN)

Scran is an educational charity providing educational access to digital materials representing Scotland's culture and history. The site contains 330,000 images, movies and sound clips from museums, galleries, archives and the media.

All local authority schools in Scotland have full access to Scran through support from the Scottish Government as do many public libraries. Most universities and colleges in Scotland also subscribe, along with a host of cultural institutions, community and home users.

The organisation was originally set up as a membership body with over 100 project partners including National Museums of Scotland, National Library of Scotland, Royal Commission on the Ancient and Historical Monuments of Scotland, Scottish Museums Council, Historic Scotland, Glasgow Museums and Art Galleries and many local collections in museums, galleries, archives and universities. Funding came from the Millennium Commission and New Opportunity Fund to enable grant-aid to organisations to permit the digitisation of national treasures.

All the resources on Scran are freely viewable up to the thumbnail level, licensed subscribers have access to the full screen sized images and the right to use the material for educational purposes.

SCRAN
Telephone: +44 (0) 131 662 1456
Email: scran@scran.ac.uk
Website: www.scran.ac.uk